*Neil
Keep shining your light.
A Emereh*

JOYOUS WEALTH
56 Secrets to Riches and Wellness

Armineh Keshishian

10-10-10
Publishing

Joyous Wealth – *56 Secrets to Riches and Wellness*
www.JoyousWealth.com

Copyright © 2020 by Armineh Keshishian

ISBN: 978-1-77277-394-1

All rights reserved. No portion of this book may be reproduced electronically, in the form of phonographic recording, stored in a data base or retrieval system, transmitted in any form or by any means, electronic, photocopying, mechanically, recording, scanning or otherwise, post it to a web site, distribute it, copied for public or private use other than for 'fair use' as brief questions embodied in articles and reviews without prior written permission of the author and the publisher as it is an infringement of the copyright law.

The content in this book has been researched. The publication is designed to provide accurate information with regard to the subject matter covered. Opinions expressed herein are only current opinions of the author, as of the date appearing in this material only and are subject to change without notice.

The opinions and information are offered in good faith and with the understanding that the author/publisher is not responsible for the results of any action taken on the basis of information in this work, nor for any errors or omissions. The author is not engaged in rendering legal, accounting, tax, investments, medical or psychological services. The book offers alternative solutions to living life joyfully; however, you must seek individual professional advice for your specific situation and circumstance in regards to financial, legal, medical and physical issues. This information is provided with the understanding that with respect to the material provided herein, you will make your own independent decision with respect to any course of action in connection herewith.

The intent of the author is only to offer information of a general nature. In the event you use any of the information in this book for yourself, which is your constitutional right, the author and the publisher assume no responsibility for your actions.

The author and publisher shall not be liable for your misuse of the enclosed material. This book is strictly for informational and educational purposes only. The purpose of this book is to educate and entertain. The author and/or publisher do not guarantee that anyone following these techniques, suggestions, tips, ideas, or strategies will become successful. The author and/or publisher shall have neither liability nor responsibility to anyone with respect to any loss or damage caused, or alleged to be caused, directly or indirectly by the information contained in this book.

Publisher: 10-10-10 Publishing, Canada
First Edition
Printed in the United States of America and Canada

Table of Contents

Foreword

D o you often wonder about your life, and how you can enhance it financially, emotionally and spiritually? Do you strive on advancing yourself to be the best you can be?

I am particularly excited to endorse this truly unique book, *Joyous Wealth – 56 Secrets to Riches and Wellness*, which encompasses concepts of wealth, mindset, empowerment, and living abundantly. The story is not only uplifting, but also a map to joy and happiness.

Armineh Keshishian is a renaissance woman who lives her life passionately and abundantly. Her accomplishments in the fields of wealth creation and management, combined with her knowledge of human behavior and psychology and her wisdom, authentic personal qualities and genuine desire, will guide you to quantum leap your life to the next level of success.

Armineh reveals the secrets to creating your desired life with practical tools that encourage you to step into your greatness. The teachings are subtle, with pragmatic application, and told in a powerful story.

This book is relevant if you are yearning for more love, more knowledge and more abundance in your life. It is a mosaic; each chapter has a specific focus, but they all fit in together perfectly.

Joyous Wealth is a rare combination of many secrets compiled together. It's a book you must have as a collectible. The information is timeless, and often refers to ancient wisdom with a modern twist.

Raymond Aaron
New York Times Bestselling Author

Message From the Author

Joyous Wealth ~ A passionate life ... A wealthy life!

Dear Reader,

I have helped many build and accelerate wealth while manifesting a joyous and successful life. Now I want to share how YOU can make YOUR dreams come true.

I decided to write this book to share my knowledge and the wisdom I have acquired over the years with YOU! I created five fictional characters based on my years of experience meeting and advising clients with diverse needs, backgrounds and status based on their age and where they were in their cycle of life. These characters all came together in order to share their lives, their stories, their knowledge, their wisdom, and their love. They felt they could make a difference based on their own experiences in life, and share the secrets embedded in the content throughout this book, inspiring you to abundance.

As a teenager, I came to Canada from the Middle East with my younger sister. It was a difficult time as we were both homesick and neither of us could speak English. However, we pressed on, went to school, adapted quickly, joined our community, and made new friends.

I look back on this time and realize all I had was Desire, Determination, and Dedication, which I call my 3D's. That was enough!

My mother was an independent woman who encouraged me to pursue higher education and be financially independent, and yet she herself was a woman of tradition. My father taught me leadership. Because I did not want to follow the traditional rules and regulations as a socially obliging Middle Eastern girl, I went on to find my own path and empowerment.

I pursued a degree in business, began working in the financial field, and built a highly successful career advising thousands of clients over the years, helping them grow their wealth significantly and live joyously. Constantly enhancing my knowledge on money matters, studying human behavior and psychology, combined with Universal Principles, provided me with a unique advantage.

I am influenced by the context of my upbringing. Being born a Christian in a Muslim country gave me extraordinary insights into different cultures, insights which help me to this day. Although cultures and values vary, I find that basic human needs, desires, and emotions are not really that different. We are one human race.

Over the years I was confronted with clients on a daily basis who were comfortable discussing not only their finances with me, but also certain intimate details of their lives. I was curious about the connection between financial well-being, success and enlightened living. Searching for truth myself and balancing my own life in the areas of physical, emotional, mental (intellectual) and spiritual aspects, I journeyed along the path to self-mastery.

Early in my career, my training in business and finance seemed to be in direct conflict with my creative, artistic self and the spiritual path I was on, exploring Universal Laws and Truth, which added an element of complexity to my understanding of life. It was only after a certain amount of integration that I felt they were all parts of me and need not be separate or conflicting. That realization was quite empowering and exciting.

I struggled my way through with passion, purpose, and persistence. Step by step I rose above adversity, challenges, and heartaches. I built my life up, with focus, excitement, and curiosity. I discovered that life is a gift, and beautiful despite the hurdles.

Combining twenty-five years of successful wealth management and financial planning in parallel with conducting 'Conscious Living' and 'Wealth Consciousness' seminars, I created a holistic approach to Wealth & Wellness for a desired life.

My intention is to inspire you to fulfill your potential. I believe living consciously is empowering, and that we have a choice in all we do. You can live your life with peace, passion and purpose, and create a fulfilling life. Your traits, attitudes, desires, determination, and commitment have a profound effect on your life. The choices you make, every day and every moment, and the thoughts you have will change the course of your life. A decision today is a road map for your future. To achieve financial wealth or comfort is possible, provided you take certain actions.

Let your passion ignite your inspired action! If you have the courage to follow your own dreams and embody your true self, I am here for you. A fulfilling and joyous life awaits!

P.S. To receive your colored copy of the *Joyous Wealth* Workbook for your personal journey, visit JoyousWealth.com.

Prologue

A few years ago, I decided to host a magnificent party at my home, inviting friends, acquaintances, and clients. Everyone accepted my invitation.

That spring evening is one I will never forget. The party was going great; some people were dancing, some others were eating, drinking, and joking around when I noticed there was a bit of commotion in the study. A group was in a deep discussion about money, which got my attention. The last thing I wanted was a dispute at the party.

I stayed quiet for a few minutes, listening and smiling until the discussion grew heated about the socioeconomics of money, women, finances, and their roles in society.

I debated whether or not to put a stop to this, but then I thought I had no right to control the discussion just because it was in my home.

Five women in the group stood out. I knew only the vaguest details about them as acquaintances:

1. Terri, CEO of a major corporation
2. Mrs. Trevor, an elderly wealthy widow
3. Sarah, a young single mom
4. Georgina, a married woman
5. Nellie, married to a very rich man

Terri was saying: "I have worked so hard to get where I am, nobody handed it to me. But then again some of my girlfriends took the easy way out. One in particular I remember married the rich businessman whom she met while we were on vacation."

I could see the emotions building up.

Nellie, married to a wealthy man, sat straight up and finally replied with poise. "I love my husband and that's why I married him."

"I am not directing my comments towards you," Terri said. "I'm simply talking about my other girlfriends who always think I got it easy, but they did not take the time to explore their potential."

Mrs. Trevor had been quiet for the longest time. At this last comment, she took a deep breath and said: "Ladies, stop it, just stop it. When you get to my age all that matters is have I made all the right choices along the way? What could I have done differently in my life? If I knew then what I know now…" A single tear came down her face.

There I was, watching it all and not knowing what to do. I really felt Mrs. Trevor's pain. I would never live my life with regret, I thought, as I am responsible for my choices today and every day. The tools I have today allow me to make wise and intelligent decisions.

The single mom, Sarah, cleared her throat and croaked: "At least one good thing I have going for me is that I am young. I certainly don't want to be in my eighties and think I made some wrong choices."

"You are never sure of your choices," Georgina finally spoke. "I have an adoring husband, beautiful children, who sometimes talk back at me." She laughed. "As much as I love them all, I still don't know what my true goals and desires are. Well, sure I can tell you what my financial goals are but emotionally I am not sure where I am or where I am going. I mean the real me. You know what I mean?" She looked at the others. "No, I guess you don't. Just forget what I said." Her face turned pale and she stared into space.

There was absolute silence in the study, as music and laughter filtered in from the other rooms.

"… emotionally not sure where I am…" kept ringing in my ears, "… emotionally not sure where I am."

I didn't ask for this! I just wanted a nice party.

The women shifted in the silence, knowing this was not the time nor the place to get into it, although everyone had a valid point to share. The conversation turned to calmer topics and I carried on to visit with the other guests.

The party ended that night leaving an unquenchable thirst in me to explore and discover more about the lives of these women. I felt an indescribable connection with them and saw the bond between all of us.

I saw their light, and the fact that we could all benefit and learn from each other's life experiences, wisdom, and vivacity. I wanted to reveal my own life experiences, knowledge and wisdom with them and uncover more about the lives of these women and their families, about their relationship to wealth, joy and success. I felt we had something special. I had felt their joy and sorrow. I couldn't stop my own tears, feeling the sadness yet strength in these women.

Since the beginning of time women have been care givers and men have been hunters. Throughout history there has been competition between women. Women who were beautiful and had physically fit bodies would attract men easily. It seems competition is genetically coded. It is also very human to feel jealous.

At the same time, as women we understand each other well and we often form friendships and groups to confide in one another and support each other. When we come together, we can move mountains.

I find human relationships fascinating. I always like to know more, and I am curious, so I pondered the dynamics of these women, the psychological and social make-up of these five women in relation to money and their families.

A few days later I decided to invite them to my home on a regular basis to have discussions on life, wealth, and joy. To my delight, they all agreed.

I was excited at the thought that all these wonderful women wanted to share and support one another. I felt we had something special here.

Our journey had only started at that party.

Chapter 1

Circle of Life! Your Life

1

The sun beamed its rays across the lake and through the living room window as all five women took their seats. Exhilaration lit me up too.

Terri sat straight in her chair, always the confident CEO. Sarah with her gorgeous green eyes and long lashes gazed at Georgina. Georgina didn't notice; she was looking down at the carpet, lost in thought.

I joyfully welcomed everyone in a bright voice. "Let's start by sharing our financial goals. Be as specific and honest as you can."

Terri didn't hesitate. "My short-term goal is to buy a new car. My medium-term goal, which is within five years, is a six-month sabbatical to tour around the world and my long-term goal is to retire in a beach house."

I looked to Sarah next. "I just wanna be rich. I'm a single mom. I wanna make sure my kid can go to college."

Nellie sighed. "I'd like to spend more time with my husband. He provides very well for me, but he works all the time."

Mrs. Trevor nodded at that. "I know the feeling, dear." She patted Nellie's shoulder, a big diamond ring on her hand. "My goal right now is to be healthy enough so I can celebrate my 85th birthday with all of my children and family. I miss my late husband so much."

Georgina still hadn't looked up, so I called on her.

"It's just…" She stared straight ahead and sighed deeply with sadness. "I wish I could have said goodbye to my mother when she died. We weren't speaking when she got ill, and she died shortly after that."

"Thank you all for sharing," I said. "I have a Four-cornerstone philosophy of life to share with you. You'll see how it connects to goals in a minute."

I took my time to explain each of the cornerstones, sometimes writing on a whiteboard I had set up beside the coffee table.

1. **Physical** aspects are anything of a physical nature related to food, shelter, our material belongings (such as a car or a house, money, wealth), our body, health, physical fitness, sex and physical relationships. These are crucial as they relate to our survival.

2. **Emotional** represents our feelings, such as happiness, anger, sadness, fear, guilt. Our perception is always based on our view of ourselves, others, and our interactions. Do we blame others, or the world for what is happening in our lives? Our emotional well-being plays a key role in our quality of life.

3. **Mental or Intellectual** is about our mind, thinking and mental capacity, and its power. It is about the intellect, creativity, mental energy and peace of mind. Reading an enjoyable book may be a stimulus to the mind. Are we focused on our goals and aspirations or scattered about our vision or the lack thereof? Clarity of our thoughts, our expectations of ourselves and others has an impact on how things come together. What do we think about or fuss about? Or do we spend time expanding our minds, learning new skills and broadening our knowledge?

4. **Spiritual** is defined differently for each person and each individual experiences it differently. It is unique to each person. Spirituality does not advocate for one specific religion, be it Christianity, Islam, Buddhism, Judaism, Hinduism. Spirituality to me encompasses my whole being, as body, mind, and spirit in connection to the Divine or the Higher Power or Life Force, or God as some people may call it.

The reason I like to distinguish each segment is that we are aware of each category and pay attention to the importance of each grouping to see how it plays a significant role in our lives.

Terri and Sarah were leaning forward, scribbling notes. Mrs. Trevor squinted, uncomfortable with the topic of spirituality. I recalled she was a devout Christian.

"Let's get more specific," I said. "My question is, do you feel connected to others, Universe, God, or do you feel separated and alone in life?"

Mrs. Trevor relaxed, and Nellie looked puzzled.

"For example," I continued, "you may be wealthy and physically fit; however, you may suffer feelings of extreme anger towards someone or some situation, and if this continues for a long period of time, it may affect you physically and start developing as sickness. This is because negative emotions produce toxins in the body regardless of how much you eat healthy food. The emotional distress causes physical upset.

"The opposite of this could also apply. You may have been very sick for a long period of time and decide that enough is enough and start using positive self-talk with the expectation that your health will improve. You may also believe in the power of prayers; therefore, you may include them in your daily routine, and after a short period of time start noticing some signs of improvement."

Georgina looked me straight in the eye. "Yeah, I can relate to that."

Everyone had found something in what I said so far, so I continued.

"When you set goals, you know which direction you're moving. You must truly know what you want in order to achieve it. In order to create your dream life, three elements are necessary for reaching your desired outcome. I call them the 3D's: Desire, Determination and Dedication. Your desire level must be hundred percent. You must really want the object of your desire otherwise you wouldn't pursue it. So for you, Sarah, how badly do you want to be rich?"

"110% desire!" she said, and everyone laughed.

"Next you must decide if you are going to do whatever it takes, and you will pursue it no matter what to get what you want. Nellie, what lengths will you go to spend time with your husband? Will you get up an hour early to prepare breakfast so you can eat together before he goes to work?"

Nellie nodded. "I want time with him, but you're right, I haven't done anything about it."

"That's a wonderful realization, Nellie. The third element is you must be totally dedicated to your goal and be willing to commit to it regardless of any challenges and foreseeable obstacles."

"That's what I'm best at," Terri said. "You should see me when I set a goal for my staff at work. Nothing can get in our way!"

"Exactly," I said. "Now, the best way is to start taking an inventory of the four cornerstones in each area to see where you are and set your intentions."

Everyone was listening intently. I asked them to name things that are important to them in relation to the four cornerstones.

One by one they mentioned the following: family; parents & children; spouse/partner; money & wealth; career/work; spirituality; religion; health; love; social network; community; fun; volunteering; vanity; friends; relationships; hobbies; travel; education; meditation; fitness/exercise; creativity; and the list went on.

"This is fantastic," I said. "Now name only five things that are truly important to you. I believe we need to look at our lives in a holistic way and decide what is important and what our priorities are. Once we give a level of importance to our goals and desires then we can work towards them."

Circle of Life

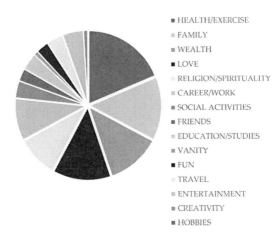

- HEALTH/EXERCISE
- FAMILY
- WEALTH
- LOVE
- RELIGION/SPIRITUALITY
- CAREER/WORK
- SOCIAL ACTIVITIES
- FRIENDS
- EDUCATION/STUDIES
- VANITY
- FUN
- TRAVEL
- ENTERTAINMENT
- CREATIVITY
- HOBBIES

It was fascinating to see how each person named their five important elements.

I wrote them on the board:

Terri: Wealth, Career, Fitness, Travel, Education
Mrs. Trevor: Family, Health, Religion, Social Network, Wealth
Sarah: Family, Love, Health, Money, Fun
Nellie: Love, Wealth, Spouse, Travel, Creativity

They were all surprised at each other's answers and how we all want different things in life.

"How's everyone doing?" I asked. "Shall we continue?"

Smiles and nods came as answers. I erased the board and drew a diagram.

Sample Wishes

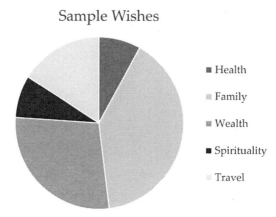

- Health
- Family
- Wealth
- Spirituality
- Travel

"Using this as an example, take a moment and write all of your wishes and dreams in the circle and give a percentage of priority in relation to the time you're willing to spend. For example, you can give 30% of your time to work to make money, 15% to spirituality, and 40% to your family, 10% to your exercise and diet, and 5% to travel based on your wishes. Then compare it to your actual time to see if you are truly doing that."

Your Wishes

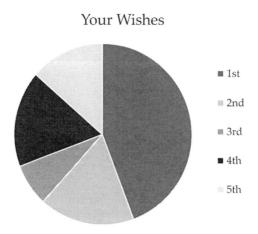

- 1st
- 2nd
- 3rd
- 4th
- 5th

Everyone was quiet and thinking about their Circle of Life.

Then Terri said: "I'm quite happy about my chart." She paused. "But I've got to say there's nothing emotional in it!" She chuckled and continued. "I don't know if this a good thing or not. I don't think about my emotions much."

Nellie gave Terri a curious look. Terri shrugged.

"We can all compare this," I encouraged. "Write down your goals and dreams and check to see where they fit in the four cornerstones as often as you can. Are you more focused on the physical aspect of your life or the spiritual aspect? Do you pay attention to your feelings? What would happen if you truly achieved your dreams? What if they came true? Day by day, if you work on your dreams, they will become a reality!"

Mrs. Trevor put her hand up, as if in class. I nodded at her.

"I know all about working day by day on your dreams. Make sure you pay attention to all the other things that are important to you too."

Sarah was pensive, far away during this exercise, but suddenly she looked at Mrs. Trevor and asked: "Like what?"

Mrs. Trevor paused. "Like your feelings, or the relationship with your children."

Nellie leaned back in her chair and started playing with her beautiful long necklace that had a large amethyst pendant.

I began: "You know, sometimes we pursue our parents' dreams. Maybe they wanted us to be the engineer or the doctor or the teacher."

"My parents wanted me to be a doctor because my father was a doctor," Nellie said. "I couldn't do it, so I studied nursing, but I never worked as a nurse."

"Life without passion or purpose is like being a machine," I said.

"You can try to please or accommodate, but this could bring feelings of guilt and resentment."

"Absolutely, I resented studying nursing all my life."

Terri looked at Nellie kindly. "Well, your parents wanted the best for you. They thought that was the appropriate choice."

Mrs. Trevor closed her eyes while shaking her head. I challenged the group. "I dare you to dream, as if there is no tomorrow. Can you take the risk? Can you take on the challenge knowing there are risks? Keep your dreams alive. Learn what is necessary and take steps to reach your destination."

Sarah almost shouted: "Oh yeah, you think it's easy? You just say do it. I don't think you know how hard it is."

I smiled. "I never said it was easy, but unless you try, you'll never know."

"Yes," Terri agreed. "That's why you need to know exactly what you want and plan for it. Start with a plan. If you could have absolutely anything you want in life, what would it be?"

"That's it," I said. "Write down whatever comes to your mind. Let's take a few minutes and do that. Then let's take a step further and look at how you see yourself in one year, in three years, in five years, in ten years, in fifteen years, and in twenty-five years. See yourself already in possession of everything you wrote down that you desire."

As they all began their lists, I continued in a soothing tone. "Can you truly see yourself owning and having everything you wrote down? How does it feel? Imagine it for a moment. If you can't see it or feel it, what is holding you back? Can you hear your thoughts? Really what are your thoughts? The big question is what would it take for you to be and have what you truly desire?

"Why do you want what you want? What does it give you? A sense of joy, happiness, serenity, peace? A sense of accomplishment, recognition, acceptance? Why is that important to you? Do you think you can achieve that sense in any other way?"

Sarah looked up. "Wow, I never thought like this before!"

"That's wonderful, Sarah." I continued: "For those of us who are old enough, let's look at where we were twenty-five years ago. What were your goals and aspirations? Did you achieve some of them at least? What experiences, life lessons and wisdom did you gain? With that in mind, can you see how powerful the next twenty-five years can be? Can you imagine it? Visualize it. What is happening in your life twenty-five years from now? Think of your relationships, your family, your money, your creativity or your career."

Everyone was writing and thinking.

Mrs. Trevor sighed. "My dear, in twenty-five years I won't be around."

"Well, what past achievements are you really excited about?"

"I seek joy. Maybe I'll share with you more another time." Then she turned to Sarah and said: "What future achievements would really excite you, Sarah? Imagine for a moment and why would they give you pleasure?"

A smile spread across Sarah's face. Nellie was beaming at her too.

Terri said: "Are you comfortable with the image in your mind?"

Sarah just looked worried and didn't say anything. A few seconds later she said: "Not all dreams come true!"

Silence drifted over the room as everyone sat quietly with their own thoughts.

Georgina hadn't said a word then volunteered to tell us about her five important wishes: "Family, Love, Health, Spouse, Money."

I was pulsating with excitement for Georgina and the rest of the group.

"If you thought about exactly what it is you wanted in life, in every area of your life, and took steps towards fulfilling your dream, there is every probability that you would reach your goal. Of course, you would face challenges and setbacks, but to keep that dream alive and never give up is the biggest joy.

"It's the journey that makes it more interesting," I said. "Success is built gradually. It's like you're at the beginning of a road; call it point A, and you want to go to point B. You either have to walk or run, but you have to travel it; you cannot get there by magic. As long as you keep your eyes on the road and finish traveling along, you will reach your destination."

The women were beaming, full of hope, and I carried on enthusiastically.

"There is a difference between being a visionary and a dreamer. If you are a visionary, it means that you have a crisp vision in your mind. You see and imagine the end result. You may not know the exact process of how to get there in order to achieve it, but you have full intention of making it happen by taking action. In order to take action, you must have the 3D's: Desire, Dedication, and Determination. You must also have the courage to see it through with intention. What is your vision? How does that feel in your heart?

"Keep your dreams alive. Learn what is necessary or the necessary steps to reach your destination.

"If you could have absolutely everything you want in life what would it be?

"You may be financially a millionaire and yet emotionally bankrupt. An acquaintance of mine once told me she was dating an extremely wealthy man and he had nothing to give her emotionally, so she called him emotionally bankrupt. When I originally heard these words, honestly I became a bit disturbed but soon found out this term was used when a person had nothing to give emotionally. It's quite disturbing to know people like this, who have suffered so much that nothing is left of their spirit.

"I know someone like that; she has suffered so much. She is as cold as ice. Nothing gets through her," Georgina added.

"There are also people who don't have much to show financially, and yet have a lot of ideas, creativity, passion, ambition, and purpose," I added.

Sarah gasped at this realization. She looked at every single person in the room to see their reaction.

I continued: "There needs to be purpose and intention behind why you want what you want. When you are inspired, the joy, the passion, and the drive come from within you."

I went on to list some of the reasons behind not feeling inspired:

1. Fear of success or failure
2. Suppressing your feelings
3. Holding on to old habits and ideas without realizing it

"In order to realize your unlimited potential, sense of self is the first place to start. 'Know thyself' gives a sense of self purpose.

"What's important now may not seem important when it's fulfilled. What is important when you're twenty is different than when you are forty."

"That is accurate," Mrs. Trevor whispered.

"One reason to know why you want what you want is to avoid excess ego and act out of inspiration," I continued.

"There's a difference between motivation and inspiration. Inspiration comes from Spirit, that we are operating 'in Spirit' instead of motives of superiority.

"Society's construct is: I am rich; I am better than you. Therefore, I can do whatever it is I want to do. The tendency to fit in may be the motivating force behind the behavior. However, if you are inspired to create a lot of wealth simply because you enjoy that game, or you help others in the process, then you are true to yourself."

Terri quickly wrote what I said and half-raised a finger. I looked at her, and she lowered it.

"The community you choose to participate in defines what you do and what you can do. Seek out a community for your needs and inspirations where you feel supported. Over time you will change communities because the nature of your needs will change. A community is the leaderless leader; a community that is strong and supportive provides a sense of wholeness."

Mrs. Trevor voiced: "I certainly need my community. Over the years I have participated in many different groups. For now, I'm content with my Church group."

As I looked around the room, I saw acknowledgements and bright, shining eyes. We all knew we were on to something great.

Chapter 2

Your Relationship with Your Self

2

We gathered two weeks later. I had prepared a variety of flavored teas and had purchased different colored markers. I asked how everyone was, as they came in one by one. I invited them to sit in the living room like last time in order to have a sense of continuity.

Mrs. Trevor was pensive. She wasn't her usual self, chatting with everyone, giving advice with love and encouragement.

The mood overall was like the day itself, gray, rainy and windy. As everyone took their seats on the loveseat, couch, and arm chairs, it felt like we had to clear the air before we could start.

"Mrs. Trevor, how are you today?" I asked.

She shook her head. "The exercise we did last time has been on my mind ever since."

"Anything in particular?"

"I never had alone time or any time for myself to see what I really wanted out of life."

Goosebumps rose on my arms. "How so?"

"There was always the children, the business, my husband, the hustle and bustle of life."

Sarah started crying. Georgina tried to hug her to calm her down, but Sarah just turned her shoulder and murmured: "Don't."

Sarah didn't seem to want to share why she felt sad.

"I can appreciate what Mrs. Trevor is saying. I'm fortunate; because I live alone, my time is my time only," Terri said. "I share it with whomever I want and whenever I want."

"Well, when you're married and have a family, you can't just think of yourself," Georgina fussed. "You've got to put food on the table, pay attention to your children and your husband. They come first; you know!"

Nellie soothed with a caring and compassionate voice. "It's nice to have alone time sometimes. Can you take a little bit of time for yourself and your self-care?"

Sarah snorted. "It's easy for you, princess! Some of us don't have that luxury."

"Darling, self-care is so important," Nellie continued. "You make time to take a bubble bath, go for a massage, relax, meditate."

Sarah glared at Nellie and turned away. Then she blurted: "Sure, I'd do all of that if I had a rich husband like you!"

Mrs. Trevor signaled Nellie not to respond to Sarah.

"Sarah, you can make money and take a couple of hours a week to take care of yourself, can't you?" Terri wondered.

"No, I can't!" she shouted at Terri. "Why does everyone fricking care about my life today?"

"We love you, honey." Mrs. Trevor reached out a hand to pat Sarah's arm, but thought better and placed it in her lap. "We don't mean to upset you."

Sarah couldn't stop crying. I sat next to her on the plush couch.

"Sarah, hold my hand." She did. "Breathe with me: inhale one, two, three. Exhale one, two, three, four, five, six. Again, inhale one, two three."

We did this for a couple of minutes until she stopped crying and started relaxing a bit.

I felt her emotions of pain, confusion, sadness, and the burden of responsibility for her child as a single parent. Sarah was only twenty years old and a sensitive soul. The breathing technique I used was to calm her; the number of inhales were half the number of exhales. I used a ratio of 1:2 for three breaths, but it could have been four or five inhales and twice as many exhales, like eight or ten.

I wanted to shake up the tension in the room. I walked towards the whiteboard in front of the wide, tall windows and said: "A question for each of you. How do you view yourself?" Everyone just stared at me.

"Have you ever considered the thoughts you have of yourself? Can you describe yourself?"

Georgina pouted.

I encouraged them to consider whether or not their thoughts were positive or negative, and offered examples:

- I am beautiful.
- I am fat.
- I can never pull this off.
- My boss does not like me.
- I am great with children.
- My spouse loves me.
- I am loveable.
- I am weak.
- I am scared.
- I can do this.
- I am capable.

- I will never be rich.
- I am sociable.

Everyone was looking at me inquisitively.

"We have 10,000 thoughts per second and our brain actually processes 1,000 thoughts per second. If you're conscious of your thoughts, you can observe them and be aware of what you think about.

"Since birth, and some even suggest before we were born, every single thought, every single observation, every single incident, word, and sentence, every single interaction with anyone and anything, every experience, impact, and every emotion has been engraved on our conscious and subconscious mind and coded and engrained in our brain. Think of time as a spiral with all thoughts and incidents on it."

I drew a spiral on the board and randomly put a few dots on each line.

"Therefore, every time we make a decision, that decision is based on all the imprints, ideas and experiences from our past. Now when we look from this point on, it encompasses all these previous imprints. These imprints are from a fraction of a second.

"What you think of yourself is the sum total of all of your experiences, thoughts, and observations. For example, if you think you are beautiful, what led you to think that? Perhaps you heard your parents say you are a gorgeous child. Or if you think you are clumsy, perhaps you picked up heavy objects when you were younger and kept dropping them, then concluded that you're clumsy."

Georgina with her short, dark, wavy hair, was eager to share. "I've always been chubby, and my mother always said, 'You have your grandmother's genes; you'll never be slim'."

"It's fascinating how we come to conclusions, how our self-image or self-worth is based on very few conversations or incidents. If you're aware of your thoughts, then moving from a negative thought process to a positive one may be beneficial."

"OK, how about: I'm never gonna be rich!" Sarah yelled.

I smiled. "You can replace this phrase with a different one if you like."

"How?" she wondered.

"When did you decide that you'll never be rich, Sarah? Did your parents tell you that?" I asked. "Or were your parents never rich, so you thought you had no chance to be rich?"

"Probably 'cause my parents weren't rich."

Georgina stretched her arms and legs while Mrs. Trevor tried a different flavored tea.

Terri finished taking notes.

"Once you are aware of your self-view you can change your thoughts. In Sarah's case, for example, regarding money, first you need to think about what rich means to you. How much money is rich? Do you define it based on your net worth or your income? Let's say you make $50,000 a year and you think rich is making $1 million a year. Or your net worth is $150,000 and you want to have $1 million of net worth.

"When you're aware of your thoughts, then you can move from a negative thought process to a positive one. Cognitive Reframing is a way to identify whether or not your thought should be reframed."

In order to expand on this approach, beside the spiral on the board, I wrote the following questions and asked the group to consider them:

1. Is my thinking based on facts?
2. Does my thinking help me achieve my goals?
3. Does my thinking help me feel the way I want to feel?

Terri raised her arm: "I believe in some cases, especially at work, my way of thinking helps me achieve my goals, but in other areas I may have conflicting thoughts."

Nellie curiously asked if Terri wanted to share. Terri hemmed and hawed.

Georgina urged: "C'mon, girl."

Terri straightened herself. "Thinking that I may never be in a committed relationship doesn't help me feel positively about that." And she stared at Georgina for a few seconds.

"I am sure you will find your match one day, a beautiful, talented and smart woman like you!" Georgina assured her.

Then I turned to Sarah. "Let's look at the phrase 'I'm never gonna be rich.' Ask yourself these three questions. If the answer to all or any of those questions is no, then replace the phrase with a different one to start conditioning your mind to open up new neuropathways. For example, you can say 'It is possible that I will be rich'. "

Sarah seemed a little more hopeful.

I have always loved the concept of 'Know Thyself' used by ancient philosophers. Everyone in the room seemed eager to learn new ideas so I suggested we try something different.

"I'll give you three different exercises which will reveal a lot about yourself."

Mrs. Trevor adjusted her glasses while Terri looked at me expectantly.

Nellie finished her tea and Sarah was quickly tapping her toe.

Exercise number #1

"How do you view yourself using body, mind, and spirit?" I went back to the whiteboard and drew a big square, a line horizontally inside middle of it and another one vertically. Then inside each of the smaller squares I wrote: physically, emotionally, mentally and spiritually.

"You can also write adjectives about yourself in those four squares. Remember: not how others see you, but how you view yourself. Any volunteers?"

Nellie indicated yes and expressed her views of herself.

PHYSICAL	EMOTIONAL
I live in a beautiful home	I am confident
I exercise three times a week	I am sensitive
I eat healthy food	I worry that I don't have a child
I don't always spend time with friends	I am kind-hearted
I think I can do more things but don't take the time	I love my husband
MENTAL/INTELLECTUAL	SPIRITUAL
I like to be stimulated therefore I read a lot of books	I meditate twice a week
I love learning	I believe in the power of life force/Universe
I am creative	
I am beautiful and sexy	
I believe in my abilities	

There were a few loud outbreaths, and Georgina said: "That's a tough one for me!"

"It's always good to take an inventory of your thoughts, see how you think of yourself and the image you hold of yourself."

"Well," Georgina shared: "I'm a wife and have two children. One of my boys is autistic. I love my husband. I work in an office. I'm trying to save for my children's education. Is that what you're asking?"

"That's a great start. Thank you for sharing, Georgina. Keep writing. In the emotional square, you might say that you are happily married to the love of your life. Under mental, do you struggle with your son's autism? Spiritually, do you feel connected to a higher power? You can then add: I am married to the love of my life, I am happy, I have a great family.

"You had said your five important elements are: Family, Love, Health, Spouse, Money.

"If you have all of those things and are satisfied then it's great but, if not, what are you doing to have what you want? How do you change your thoughts? Are you healthy? Is that a concern for you? Or emotionally, are you happy or sad? You had said you felt regret not speaking with your mother before she passed away. This is the specific type of inventory."

Georgina took a deep breath and continued: "Well I am 30 pounds overweight; I don't have enough money to do the things I want although both my husband and I work. Yes, I am devastated about my mom. One of my children is mentally challenged and it is very difficult." She paused and said in a loud, sad voice: "Is this what you're talking about?"

I made a chart for Georgina to illustrate and asked her if she could think of positive attributes.

PHYSICAL	EMOTIONAL
I am 30 lbs. overweight I don't have enough money to do the things I want	I am devastated about my mom One of my children is mentally challenged and it is very difficult I am married to the love of my life I am happy, I have a great family
MENTAL/INTELLECTUAL	SPIRITUAL

"Everyone, the idea here is to count our blessings, express gratitude for what we have, and take an inventory of what is troubling us so we can deal with the challenges in order to have a better quality of life with more peace and more joy."

Georgina blinked in disbelief and did not say anything.

Terri turned to her with a hint of envy. "Georgina, you're married and have a great family. Why are you so sad?"

"Giving gratitude is one way to increase your peace of mind and elevate your life," Mrs. Trevor offered.

"I'm not complaining. I'm just saying how my life is," Georgina replied.

Terri perked up. "Well that's great. That's exactly what we're talking about."

I enjoyed seeing Mrs. Trevor tasting all different flavors of tea I had put on the coffee table. I asked everyone to try the assorted pastries. Georgina loved the chocolate one and Terri tried the berries. It had stopped raining and the clouds had started to part.

While Sarah was getting a glass of water she burst out: "I am thankful for my daughter Anusha. She is my life. I got pregnant when

I was a teenager, and her father didn't want anything to do with me. I have a girlfriend now and we're thinking about living together!"

"You mean common-law? Without marriage?" Nellie asked.

"You have a problem with that?" Sarah glared.

"Oh no, not at all," Nellie assured her. "It was just a question. I envy your love for your daughter, Sarah. My husband and I always wanted our own children, but we were never blessed."

Sarah coughed a couple of times looking at Nellie: "I've had a rough childhood so excuse me if I'm resentful about you living like a princess."

Although Nellie sounded compassionate, she told her: "I believe in what I want and how I like to live my life. Isn't that what we are talking about?"

Sarah lashed out: "Yea, the view I hold of myself isn't rosy like you ma'am."

Georgina gestured palms up. "You are beautiful, Sarah, and have a child. You must be happy, no?"

"I am happy about having my daughter. She is everything to me, but I don't have any money, and my girlfriend is constantly lecturing me to give up drugs. You can say I view myself as an addict."

Sarah's eyes opened wide as her words had just slipped out and she realized she may have said too much.

Nellie asked with a surprise: "How come you do drugs?"

"It's none of your business, lady!" Sarah screamed.

"Ladies," I said, bringing us back to the topic at hand. "The reason behind this exercise was to consider how we view ourselves, the belief systems we have about our own selves and what we want to change. Perhaps you can think about this a little more on your own. Let's have more tea and then we'll continue."

Everyone agreed except Sarah, who stormed out to have a smoke.

After twenty minutes of light chatter and some laughter in the kitchen, we decided to go back to the living room to continue our discussion. Sarah was watching from the backyard and joined us.

I began by writing on the board:

Exercise number #2

"The second exercise is to discover your core characteristics, which are your character strengths and your divine gifts."

Mrs. Trevor offered a big smile and affirmed: "I can see you all have so many gifts."

"Like what?" Sarah asked hesitantly.

"You, my dear, have so much love to give. You are compassionate even though you are hurting." Mrs. Trevor continued with Terri. "You have leadership qualities and are a problem solver."

Georgina sniped: "What, are you a psychic now?"

"No," Mrs. Trevor chuckled, "just stating the obvious."

"Mrs. Trevor, you are one wise, just and articulate woman," I proclaimed. "And you, Nellie, are a beautiful soul."

"We all have gifts we are born with. These gifts are embedded in our characters and personalities. I find it inspiring to explore our natural strengths in order to live a more fulfilling life. By recognizing our signature strengths, we can flourish much faster. It is important to recognize that skills are learned whereas characteristics are natural attributes. For example, two people may learn to speak a new language; one can speak the language fluently and without any accent in a short period of time whereas the other may take much longer to learn and still struggle with the accent, assuming both spent the same amount of time and effort learning the new language. It's fair to say one is naturally better at learning a new language than the other. In a different scenario, the same person with a flair and ability to learn new languages may be less prudent in decision making. With effort you can increase your skills; however, your natural gifts and strengths are innate. Oftentimes in the business world the tendency is to focus on one's weaknesses in order to excel; however, the joyful way is to focus on your strengths and learn what is necessary to propel.

"Let's explore this concept by sharing our strengths from a place of who we truly are and not how we view ourselves. I can go first." I saw grins all around.

"I naturally have a lot of energy. I am positive and hopeful. I always take a look at the bigger picture. I can see different perspectives on the same issue. I am Spiritual and easily connect to universal forces, and I have the ability to bring a lot of people together who are on the same wavelength. I have not learned these anywhere and yet I am capable of all that."

"I am enthralled," Terri complimented. "I am a natural leader; thank you Mrs. Trevor for seeing that in me. I am naturally persistent and always have an open mind before I judge anything. As you said, I have not learned these characteristics anywhere."

"Sarah, can you think of any of your natural strengths?" Nellie asked.

Sarah shrugged while Georgina interjected: "I am naturally great with children and I am very honest."

I felt overjoyed witnessing them beginning to see their greatness.

Exercise number #3

"The last exercise today is tapping into your Inner Wisdom. Before we dive into this topic, I'd like to explain the three sections of our brain and how they function."

Again, I used the whiteboard while I spoke.

"First is the lizard brain. It automatically takes care of bodily functions, things we don't normally think about like digesting food or breathing.

"Second is the limbic or animal brain. The limbic system, also known as the mammalian brain, has four functions or the 4 F's: fight, flight, freeze, and fornicate. This section of the brain also creates emotions and memories. When we feel fear or stress, our limbic brain thinks we need to kick into survival mode. It approaches things that are good and stays away from bad. The more decisions we make this way, the stronger the limbic brain gets.

"Lastly, we have the evolutionary brain, the neocortex, also known as the thinking brain. To boost this thinking or rational brain, we must practice thinking instead of constantly feeling we are in fight or flight mode, which is survival mode.

"The key is to pay attention to our reactions because only the limbic or rational brain can take charge. As I just said, if we use the limbic brain all the time, it gets stronger. Instead we can attempt to use the rational or evolutionary brain."

I noticed Sarah sitting on the edge of her seat and listening intently. Nellie was playing with her necklace and writing key words in her notes.

"As you become more familiar with the different brain functions, you become more aware of your actions and reactions, and can develop knowledge and skills that add to your experiences and wisdom. In order to tap into your wisdom, you must have peace of mind. When you have more peace of mind and are not in fight or flight mode, you can access information that normally would not be available to you.

"Peace of mind does not mean you do not have challenges or that you are always in a positive state of mind. It just means you are at peace with yourself to do the tasks at hand and deal with the challenges you face. Peace of mind requires you to be and act without giving into fear.

"When you are stressed or in fear you default to the limbic brain, and it thinks you need to kick into survival mode. Relaxation tells the limbic system to stay out of survival gear. Then the body is not in a fight, flight or freeze mode. Oxycontin, dopamine and serotonin start flowing freely through the body and can give a sense of peace.

"This means you need to reduce your mind chatter, take care of your physical body and your emotions. Sources of depletion may include stress, pain, constantly making decisions (resulting in decision fatigue), taking difficult initiatives, multi-tasking, restraining impulses, sleep deprivation, and using substances like drugs and alcohol."

"I know all about decision fatigue," Terri interjected. "I'm constantly making decisions at work. I'm always evaluating the pros and cons of my decisions and making sure I have made the right ones. It's exhausting."

Mrs. Trevor agreed. "When you constantly make business decisions, it takes a toll on your mind and your body."

Sarah looked puzzled. I nodded for her to voice her question.

"Are you saying substance use depletes you?" She hesitated and then shrugged again. "I feel good doing drugs."

"When we're depleted, it's hard to excel and be joyful," I added. "I know a few successful people who are constantly running on low energy. My guess is one of these days they will burn out. And then again I know a lot of successful people who make it a priority to replenish by exercising, meditating, and taking care of themselves. Good sleep and proper nutrition are a must. In addition, relationships that are important to us and bring a lot of joy, bring emotional nourishment."

"I can attest to that!" Mrs. Trevor agreed. "My husband and I had each other. He had a great sense of satisfaction having me by his side, supporting him even when we had challenges."

"My husband works hard and exercises every morning. I always prepare good, nutritious food for us, and I want him to start mediating." Nellie smiled. "Sometimes he does."

I loved that everyone was enjoying the conversation.

"Using relaxation techniques reduces limbic reactions to stress, which increases peace of mind. When you meditate, you must be in a relaxed state. That is when you can be creative, get answers and solutions to problems you are facing, and access your Inner Wisdom. The answers lie within you if you only believe that and listen! You know what is best for your life!"

"I know this type of exercise will take a long time to develop. Can we continue with our discussion and take up this topic some other time?" Nellie asked.

Everyone agreed . It was time to review where we were. We'd discussed a lot in one day.

"Earlier we talked about how every single thought, every single observation, incident, word, sentence, and interaction with anyone about anything has been engraved on our conscious and subconscious mind." I continued: "Then we discussed the three sections of the brain.

"Another important fact must be addressed. There is the unconscious mind, then the subconscious mind, and the conscious mind sits on top. Our conscious mind is aware of our thoughts; it is the cognitive mind. The subconscious mind is all the recorded impressions, and the unconscious mind is where the invisible and the unknown exists."

Georgina and Mrs. Trevor looked skeptical but interested in what I was saying.

Terri said: "Fascinating."

"I've heard of these concepts, but I don't think science has proven them all." Nellie shared her doubts.

"Not quite, Nellie." I continued: "I love these topics on metaphysics and Universal Principles. Just because we can't see them doesn't mean they don't exist. I can assure you a lot of our behaviors stem from our subconscious. In addition, through practice and meditation, we can access the unconscious. We can discuss this another time as well. I just wanted to bring the subject to your attention."

Nellie nodded.

I was inspired and said: "To wrap up today's discussion is to know that our traits, attitudes, passion, determination, and commitment will have a profound effect on our lives. Choices are made each moment. The choices we make every day, every moment, and the thoughts we have will change the course of our lives. Any decision you make today is a road map for your future. Moment by moment you create and construct your life!"

"Amen to that!" Sarah cheered.

I was happy to see that everyone was open-minded enough to take on the new information and was willing to look at life with a new perspective.

"Last time we talked about the 3D's: Desire, Determination and Dedication, and today we talked about how we view ourselves, the images we hold of ourselves and our natural strengths. I now encourage you to Make Your Declaration to move you to a joyful place!"

I offered an example:

I declare that I am __*hopeful about the future*___ and desire _*to share my wisdom and knowledge* __ and will do/be _*build a community of like-minded individuals* _ to live a fulfilled life!

Everyone was animated, we finished our session on a positive note, and said we would come back the following week with all the day's exercises done. Then we hugged each other good night.

Chapter 3

Your Passion, Your Purpose

3

I was looking forward to seeing everyone when we met a week later. The women seemed to be in a good mood, chatting while we sat in our usual place in the living room. I asked whether they had thought about the exercises we discussed and if they actually did the assignments. They all confirmed they had. Then I asked if they had any questions. They agreed it was work in progress and they would continue working on the exercises and realizations.

Then I posed a question: "What brings you joy?"

A smile captured their faces.

"Today we will talk about passion, purpose and creativity. If you had all the wealth in the world, what kind of work would you do?"

Everyone perked up.

"What is your passion? Dancing, nursing, teaching, carpentry, business? Can you clearly state what kind of occupation you love?"

Georgina burst out: "I love designing and decorating."

"That's awesome Georgina! Are you taking time for yourself to pursue your interest or are you too busy working to the point of exhaustion, especially when you have to take care of your home, your spouse, your children and housework?"

Georgina threw her hands in the air as Nellie anxiously waited to hear her response.

"Let's assume you have enough money and live very comfortably. What's next?" I asked.

Mrs. Trevor looked up as if to say something but stopped.

I continued: "In order to create joy the first thing you may consider doing is to decide what really inspires you and what you are passionate about. If time and money were not an issue, what would you love to do? Paint, sing, coach, design, write, be an engineer, a digital marketer?"

Nellie's perfume was intoxicating. She looked classy, gorgeous and sensuous. With her dreamy eyes she shared: "I practice yoga, take care of my home, study metaphysics." She paused, and then continued: "and go shopping. Mrs. Trevor, you had mentioned that you seek joy; would you like to share?"

Mrs. Trevor looked into the air. "Maybe a little later. But you are joyful!"

Nellie nodded.

"If not joyful, what is holding you back from satisfying your passion?" I asked. "Money and time are obstacles you can overcome. Are you committed to pursuing what you are passionate about?"

"It's too late for me now!" Mrs. Trevor responded.

"For now think about what you would have wanted, Mrs. Trevor," I said.

"If you are not sure, you may start writing a few things you absolutely love. Let's say working with children, or math and science, or exercising, travelling, being outdoors. Once you start writing everything you love to do you will find a common thread that may lead you to a particular occupation."

"I love to dance, but I never had the money to take ongoing classes. Then I got pregnant with my baby. But in reality if I had a chance I would wanna study law," Sarah shared.

"Interesting," Terri added. "I love sports. I go to the gym four times a week and play squash twice a week. I'm quite interested in wood carving."

Georgina said: "I would love to be a decorator, but I can't with work and family. I have no time to do anything. Once in a while I read books on psychology."

"I'd love to be an opera singer, but I would never dream of pursuing it. It's really frowned upon in our culture," Nellie murmured.

Mrs. Trevor crossed her legs: "I wanted to be a ballerina!"

Everyone looked at her with surprise.

She inhaled and exhaled slowly. "No one could do such a thing back then. To be a dancer, oh no, it was not acceptable. Instead I married the boy next door and had my family. I was too young when we married. I didn't know much about anything. He was a boy from a nice family. He always brought me roses."

"Aw, isn't that romantic!" Nellie cooed.

"I was a shy girl at sixteen. He fell in love with me and I was in love with his kindness."

A moment of awe filled the room.

"Right now, I'm passionate about my church but if I was to do anything creative I would want to write about my life and share it with the world," Mrs. Trevor continued.

"Mrs. Trevor, what would you write about specifically?" I asked.

She replied with a sad voice: "My heartaches. I've endured a lot but most importantly I survived with passion, perseverance and patience."

"I'm blown away," Sarah declared.

"I understand the perseverance it takes," I stated. "We must be passionate instead of doing things that come from a place of fear or self-imposed obligation. An example may be when we follow what our parents want us to do, or better yet what our culture dictates we do or be, with the expectation of following the rules."

"It's unfortunately a problem in many cultures," Terri sighed.

"I think most people get carried away with their work and life and everything becomes routine. There is no time for anything else. But it looks like the younger generation is more apt to be creative. I guess parents help children become more creative," Georgina said.

Nellie had a distant look in her eyes. "Well, you know having money and actually lots of it is great, but to sacrifice joy, health and a life missed of happiness is not really fulfilling." She played with her wedding ring. "When you spend all your time making money. I'm not suggesting you don't think about money and the comfort it brings. You can be happy and wealthy but don't miss out on the rest of what life has to offer or what you have to offer life."

"I love that phrase, Nellie. Certain elements are powerful motivators," I said. "Joy comes when you are following your passion and your dreams and when you have a purpose."

Georgina crossed her arms. "So what I hear you say is to find your passion and pursue it regardless of challenges?"

I smiled with a nod. Then I challenged them to think about some questions which I wrote on the board:

1. If you had money, would you continue doing exactly what you are currently doing?
2. If you did not have the money that you now have, would the people around you still talk to you and be friends with you?"

Mrs. Trevor uncrossed her legs. "In the beginning I had to work to help out my husband. I often worked part time; sometimes in a grocery store, sometimes in a flower store and later on, at the library. You've got to do what it takes. Those were the good old days. I was married to him for 65 years. That's a lifetime."

She looked so beautiful, so pure and loving.

"As much as I loved and respected my husband, at times I would get fed up with his behavior. I had a lot of energy. I walked every day, took care of the children and the household. I would normally sleep only five to six hours a day."

"That's beautiful," Terri said. "I always ask my team at work if they're doing anything to move closer to their goals or as you say to their desired activities. Let's say they would love to be a singer, are they taking classes? Or are they writing music? They may say they don't have time or are too old or they don't know what they want. I say take one step at a time. If they know how to play a musical instrument and would like to be in a band, they can start by getting into a local one, do gigs and create some extra income for themselves or they can start teaching how to play a musical instrument and charge for their time."

I intercepted: "Or you might have studied law because your family wanted you to be a lawyer but you actually love being a chef! Well then you may pursue cooking, learn about different dishes, work part time as a chef and see how everything goes."

"Exactly" Terri leaned forward.

I continued: "To achieve success requires responsibility, accountability and a truck load of passion and determination. Once you

45

find your passion you must determine what the purpose is. You may search for your purpose in life and not know the answer. Some are lucky to find their purpose along with their passion and some follow their passion without focusing on purpose."

Georgina looked at me curiously.

"Courage plays an important role in following your passion," I added.

Sarah was scribbling notes when she suddenly looked up as if she had a question. I signaled her to go ahead.

"Ok so if I have the 3D's of Desire, Determination and Dedication, I have to make sure my passion is my desire? And then have courage?"

"Excellent question, Sarah. I define desire under the subcategory of passion. You may have a desire to travel to an exotic destination or have a desire to take dance classes, but you are passionate about dance and become a dancer or a performer. In order to become a performer, you must have courage to take the necessary steps."

"Courage is key," Mrs. Trevor confirmed.

"Absolutely, everything starts with a dream and a vision. It may be financial success or artistic excellence to be an accomplished violin player or a world class opera singer. It takes courage to reach success," I explained. "So far we've talked about having a dream, a vision, or a goal. We must look at our life in the four cornerstone context and our life chart, to see how they all fit together. Your purpose and intention must be absolutely clear. Once we know why we strive to have or be whatever it is, then we have the path ahead of us. We consciously and intentionally shift our way of thinking to believing that it is possible, and we walk the path. It takes conscious effort."

Terri is of mixed European heritage, tall, light complexion with high cheek bones and mesmerizing blue eyes. She said: "True. I remember I was six years old. I went out with my father once and we briefly met his friends and colleagues. My father introduced me and I shook each of their hands with a smile. I remember what an incredible feeling that was; to be a little girl in the grownups' world." She leaned back in her chair, put her hands behind her head and continued: "That was a defining moment for me."

She paused with a beautiful smile.

"I made a decision at that time to be part of a man's world. It felt good to be acknowledged by men who dominated the world; as an equal. I am now the CEO of a multi-million-dollar company and have the respect of my colleagues and my team. But it wasn't easy getting there; I faced a lot of challenges along the way."

Sarah complained: "Wow! I wish my father did that."

"You know, Sarah, you can still follow your passion; it's not too late. You are young and have your whole future ahead of you."

Sarah shrugged. "Maybe."

Terri hesitated while stroking her hair. "When I was a little girl I used to imagine that I had a job with quite a bit of freedom. I imagined I made a lot of money and was always happy, partying," she said.

"Partying? You don't seem to be the type." Georgina laughed.

"I used to play hard and work hard when I was younger. Believe me, but not much anymore; I guess my priorities have changed," Terri replied.

Nellie and Georgina were smiling.

I was impressed by Terri's story. "Your passion was ignited by that defining moment which had a profound impact on you."

Terri agreed.

"You had the courage to pursue your dream and most importantly you believed in yourself," I added.

"I did, because I held on to the memory of that excitement," Terri said joyfully.

"We talked about the difference between a dreamer and a visionary. Imagine… Your most precious dream! Can you see it? Can you feel it? Do you have the courage to follow your dream?"

I noticed sparkling eyes throughout the room.

"If you just dream, your desires may remain in your heart and your mind, but if you are a visionary it means you take action and make your dreams reality. When your passion and determination are strong and fueled by courage there is no limit to what you can achieve."

They were captivated.

"Think of your most precious desire, your unfulfilled dream. Do you have the courage to pursue it or will you let it be locked in your heart?"

"It takes courage to be a visionary," Georgina repeated, deep in thought.

I continued: "According to Merriam Webster dictionary Courage means the mental or moral strength to resist opposition, danger, or hardship. Courage implies firmness of mind and will in the face of difficulty. It comes from the Latin word *cor* which means heart. Some synonyms for courage are boldness, tenacity, fearlessness, audacity, bravery, determination, daring.

"Another reason most people don't follow their vision is because of fear."

Sarah leaned back in her chair, crossing both her arms and legs.

"I want to share with you some fears I faced many years ago." I paused and then listed some of the fears I had read, which we all face:

1. Fear of old age
2. Fear of criticism
3. Fear of poverty
4. Fear of not being loved
5. Fear of bad health
6. Fear of death

"At the time I was in great physical shape. I was loved by my family, friends and my boyfriend at the time. I had money. I was young and didn't fear death. And frankly, I couldn't care less what anyone thought of me. After reading the list, I thought, really? These fears? bring them on!

"Oh, what a request. I will never forget that time. Universe really showed me what it's like to be fearful. I felt all of those fears together at the same time! Can you imagine? All together, not one at a time! I went through a very difficult time facing my fears and trying to deal with them. It was almost paralyzing."

"What did you do?" Sarah uncrossed her arms and legs and leaned forward.

"I was in fear imagining my future, having no money, old and gray, all alone and sick. I couldn't get those thoughts out of my mind. I thought I would die without joy. I didn't have the tools then to stop my thoughts. I didn't make any important decisions; however, I did ask the Universe to please stop the madness. I got its message. I asked the Universe to please teach me gently and one lesson at a time if it needs to teach."

"I am speechless," Mrs. Trevor signed with relief.

I shook my head and continued: "It is awful to live in fear. I was fortunate Universe heard me. I was able to embrace my fears slowly and move on. Although the fears felt real, I didn't have any reason to believe that my imagined future would be real."

I felt everyone's eyes on me.

"Most of the time fear keeps us from getting what we truly want. We don't follow our passion because of fear of some sort. Fear of poverty is a real fear that stops us from following our heart. Fear is the need for survival; the limbic brain trying to protect us. There are of course other fears such as fear of loneliness, of public speaking, of heights, of small spaces and many more."

Sarah cleared her throat. "My fear is not being able to hold a job 'cause of my drug use and fear of losing Anusha."

"That's understandable, Sarah; you'll figure it out." Mrs. Trevor patted Sarah's hand.

"I hope so!" Sarah blurted.

"I like to share another concept with you," I said cheerfully.

Nellie and Terri encouraged me at the same time. "Please go ahead."

"Have you ever thought about Joy of Death? Sense of Life?" I asked with a smile.

Mrs. Trevor tilted her head and adjusted her glasses. "Not at all, tell me more."

I took a few sips of water.

"I find the words compelling and thought-provoking! When I originally heard those words, I didn't know what to make of them, but they kept coming to my mind day after day. Is it about dying? Is it about living? What is it all about? Then I decided I was going to interpret the phrase with a sense of empowerment and a sense of being in charge of life and finances. Joy of Death may be a sense of fulfillment when we die, or perhaps feeling the death of our old self and the birth of our new and improved self."

"What do you mean?" Georgina asked curiously.

"For example, when we talk about wealth, we can assume death of a self that perhaps was too frivolous, or too selfish, or too guilty to enjoy life with money saved through hard work, and the birth of a new and improved self. A new self that agrees to go on that dream vacation it never thought possible. Another example of a new self may be one who gave up habits such as excessive drinking, smoking or gambling that could have caused family wounds, wasted precious time and money, a self that would save the house which might have been repossessed by creditors."

Sarah poured more water in her glass and stood up.

I continued: "Think of a set of behaviors that are not working for you, such as always attracting chaotic relationships to your life. Death of this self is possible when you decide you will not participate in those relationships. Then you embrace your new self and begin attracting healthy and joyous relationships."

Georgina fixed the collar of her blouse and massaged her temple. "So death of a fearful self or a self that lacks courage can increase passion and help you become more courageous to follow your dreams?"

"Precisely," I responded. "Life is an endless cycle just like the four seasons; after winter comes spring. Sense of Life can be construed as a sense of release after the Joy of Death. Sense of Life can be a breath of fresh air where everything is crisp and crystal clear. It could mean you know what you want in life, you have a purpose and a sense of well-being. You feel prosperous and believe everything is possible!"

They all seemed to be reflecting so we decided to take a short break and Sarah went out for a quick smoke.

When we resumed, I stood next to the whiteboard referring to the content: "We have talked about our passions and highlighted some fears. A few other ones may be fear of losing a child, losing a job, losing status or losing a spouse."

Mrs. Trevor sat straight in her arm chair, made a pyramid with her hands and in a firm voice expressed: "My husband Gabby worked day and night for fifteen years to put food on the table. After years of struggle, one day he told me he wanted to open his own business. I looked at him with worry, unsure what to say. We had just lost our boy Antonio."

We all gasped as Mrs. Trevor paused and took a breath.

Sorrow took over the room. I noticed goosebumps on Sarah, Georgina and myself.

"Gabby was already working long hours. I suppose he was having a hard time coping with the loss of our son, so he put all his time and energy into the new business. He said: 'We are gonna make it. I can do this.' I knew he could; he spoke with conviction and determination. I told him I would support him."

Georgina sighed heavily. "There are no words to comfort one who has lost a child."

Mrs. Trevor swallowed, took another deep breath and stared far in the distance.

Nellie said: "Life is precious, we can't take it for granted."

"It sure is," Sarah burst out sadly.

"I am not afraid of death," Mrs. Trevor continued. "I have lived a good life even if I could have done some things differently. We had seven children. My Antonio died at the age of four."

An unbearable silence embraced the room.

"I was devastated." Tears rolled down her cheeks. "That was a long time ago."

Mrs. Trevor was trying so hard not to cry, covering her mouth. She inhaled deeply again.

"My little angel," she cried quietly.

We all felt her pain. Nellie had her hands in prayer in front of her mouth while Terri kept breathing to calm herself.

"My son Antonio died of polio..." She rubbed her temples. "It happened so fast; we didn't know how he contracted it. Doctors tried everything, but they couldn't save him. I was crushed. I couldn't talk about it for many years." She put a hand on her heart to compose herself. "My husband put all his focus on his work."

Her pain had captured our breath. With teary eyes, Nellie kept biting her lips. Georgina kept rubbing her hands and snuffling.

"I loved that boy so much; he was always smiling, laughing and running around. He would say, 'Mommy, Mommy, come see what I built!'." Another tear fell off her cheek. She was yearning. "I cried and cried but nothing changed. I was so disappointed with life, with myself, with certain members of my family, but there was nothing I could do." She paused and clasped her hands. "Eventually I accepted the fact that maybe it was his destiny."

Sarah went to sit next to Mrs. Trevor and cried in a broken voice: "I can't fricking imagine what that must have been like."

Mrs. Trevor let out a long exhale. "Take a good care of your daughter."

"I'm afraid I'm gonna die of an overdose and leave Anusha on the streets."

Sarah was a restless soul. I wanted to hug her, give her comfort and tell her that it may be just a fear. I wanted to tell her that she loved her little girl too much to let that happen.

Terri was quiet with almost no expression. She mumbled: "I'm afraid I'm going to die with no one by my side."

For the first time she had lost her poise and confidence.

Georgina immediately followed. "I'm afraid my husband is gonna leave me." She paused. "We were ahead of our time, you know. We lived together before we were married. It wasn't acceptable back then, but we had to try." She blushed. "Sex was great, but I had to make sure living with him would be great as well. We're getting older and have children, so we're not that intimate anymore. I'll go nuts if I have to take care of my two boys by myself."

"I think I am afraid to get some sort of disease or illness," Nellie expressed. Everyone looked at her, confused. "Just in case my husband is cheating on me."

"Why do you think that?" Georgina asked.

Nellie sighed. "I don't know."

"While it's important to be aware of our fears, care must be exercised not to let imagination fuel our fears," I said.

Mrs. Trevor cleared her voice. "When you spoke about Joy of Death it reminded me of Antonio's death. But we were speaking about passion and perseverance. I wanted to share that my husband turned his grief and sadness into passion and put all his energy into the business."

"That can work like magic sometimes," Terri agreed.

"Indeed," I continued. "Passion and grief may be opposite ends of the spectrum. To follow your passion takes a lot of guts, courage and determination. After taking the first steps towards your vision, doubts may enter your mind, making you question whether or not you made the right decision. Was the decision to take time away from your family to pursue your dreams the right choice? Or did you make the right decision thinking you could manage the challenges ahead? You may question whether you have what it takes to reach the finish line."

"My husband was determined and dedicated first, which are in reverse order of Desire, Determination and Dedication. His passion was to move away from grief," Mrs. Trevor explained.

"I understand. Fear, lack of courage or belief in yourself are some of the main obstacles," I explained. "Courage brings confidence and self-belief will help you resolve challenges quickly by learning what is needed and adapting to change. It is delightful to be engaged in the process and the journey deepens us."

Terri attested: "I know exactly what you're saying. I see it at work all the time."

"In some cases you may wish a hero could just come along and make you successful or make your dreams come true," I added. "It's important to pay attention to your thoughts and expectations. Never give up hope. Always reach for your dreams and get want you want in life. You deserve it. Live the potential you, the happy you. To me life is like a grocery store. When you go shopping, you don't pick up everything in the store; you pick what you want or need. Do the same with your life and never let anyone tell you that you can't because if you can think it, and you believe in it, you will achieve it."

Nellie was observing Mrs. Trevor, who sat absorbing it all. I continued.

"Now the issue becomes how you gather the courage to do the things you truly want. One answer I have found is to be true to yourself. The ultimate betrayal would be to think you could have reached your dreams and goals and desires, and did not, because you didn't feel strong enough or fear got the best of you. These are legitimate reasons, there is absolutely no question about that. However, to give in to these negative feelings, to not stretch our limits and see the many possibilities available, is the true tragedy."

"I totally agree." Terri's voice was passionate.

I smiled. "Where do we get the courage needed to follow our dreams? Courage is one of the most important virtues in life. Courage comes by taking the first step. You take a step and then another and another. As you progress, you add to your experience and build your confidence.

"Can you see the beauty in your experience? What was your part in it? Can you see it? How did you contribute to the experience?

"As your experience and confidence grow, you take more steps and bigger steps and eventually you get there."

Positive energy emanated from everyone. Terri told us that discussing passion, overcoming fears and challenges, being courageous and taking steps to reach our dreams while believing in ourselves was empowering.

The sun set behind the glorious blue waters of the lake. That day we had shared our fears, laughed and cried. It was time to call it a night. We said we would reconvene some other time.

* * *

Days went by and I kept thinking about Mrs. Trevor before we met again. I thought about her loss and her resiliency. I remembered how she would often smile and say: "Your 3D's and my 3P's of Passion, Perseverance and Patience."

Mrs. Trevor called two weeks later and suggested we meet at her house. She invited us for a special lunch. We all agreed.

It was a beautiful day; the rain had cleaned the air fresh on a Saturday. As I approached the gate, I was greeted warmly by the concierge through the intercom. I proceeded to drive in and I took in the beauty of the garden with luscious trees and breathtaking colorful flowers. I parked my car on the massive, long driveway. As I stepped out I inhaled the blissful fragrance of gardenia, hyacinth, lilac and roses. What a beautiful sight! Terri and Nellie pulled in right behind me. Georgina had picked up Sarah and they arrived momentarily.

We rang the doorbell, which sounded rich and regal. A well-dressed maid opened the door with: "Mrs. Trevor is expecting you!" Behind her we saw Mrs. Trevor with a big smile: "Welcome, welcome, please come in." We all hugged her and thanked her for the invitation. Her house was so beautiful, with thirty-foot ceilings, a foyer, open concept, airy and welcoming. She lived there with her maid and the maid's husband.

We sat in the kitchen, which could entertain at least fifty people comfortably. Mrs. Trevor had a big family, and she was truly happy to see us there. We enjoyed the delicious lunch prepared for us, talking, laughing and telling stories.

Sarah finally asked: "Mrs. Trevor, how does one afford to live a life of this luxury?"

Mrs. Trevor put her elbows on the table, clasped her hands and smiled.

"Hard work, perseverance and surrounding yourself with the right people."

"How?" Sarah asked curiously.

"When my husband decided to open the business after Antonio died," Mrs. Trevor paused, "we had saved and invested some funds, borrowed some more from the bank and registered a corporation. He started a heating and air conditioning business with one shop and expanded to a few more within five years. We were fifty-fifty partners, but he took care of everything. We had a knowledgeable and trustworthy team who advised us on accounting, tax issues and legal matters.

"My husband Gabby had a way with people; he was always respectful to everyone. He was mild mannered and gave people a chance to excel. He hired the best people and created a pleasant and profitable work place. The employees loved him dearly. He told them what the job requirements and expectations were and offered a profit share. You cannot reach the pinnacle of success by yourself."

Sarah and Nellie were captivated. Terri listened enraptured.

"How many employees do you now have, Mrs. Trevor?" Georgina asked.

"Over a thousand," she replied.

We had talked about passion and purpose, and since Mrs. Trevor's husband had turned his emotional bruise into something positive I thought it was a great time to talk about how to make big things happen faster. When I asked the group, their eyes lit up with excitement.

"In order to make big things happen faster the first step is to normalize the big thing, normalize the life that you choose. For example, you may want to have tremendous amount of wealth, create a specific community, start a global business, build a hospital or a private school. Therefore you normalize it."

Terri and Sarah looked startled, while Georgina calmly finished her dessert.

"Mrs. Trevor, I understand your husband may not have originally set out to create this big thing; however, I am sharing the approach of how to make it possible. After you normalize it then you ask why is it a big thing? And why do you want the big thing? Because you believe it to be big, that can lead to achieving it."

Mrs. Trevor signaled the maid to clear the table and looked at me.

"Yes, I agree, and many years later I thought the business was a big thing which ultimately led us to achieve success."

"Exactly," I agreed. "You consider it big because you are not there yet! This thought process can momentarily adversely affect your perception. If you can see that big thing and make it to be four smaller things you can actually attain it."

Mrs. Trevor shared that she was not exactly sure how the process had worked since her husband was the force behind their company. Terri was looking at me intensely, waiting for my every word.

"When you are constructing a blueprint for that big thing you intend to accomplish, make it the biggest thing and divide it into four things, then separate those and have each one be a personal accomplishment. Our brain can do three things, but four confuses the brain so it separates the now from the future. This fourth part can involve someone else and it will bring hope; it allows for collaboration and participation."

"We can then conclude that big things always take collaboration with others," Terri claimed.

Mrs. Trevor and Nellie agreed. I continued.

"Then in turn you can divide each part into four smaller parts to make it easier. The main element to remember is the number four: always divide each segment into four to make it smaller and smaller, to make it manageable and achievable."

Terri jumped right in: "I am indeed fascinated by this concept. Can you elaborate please?"

"Of course," I continued. "Make small things more plentiful, things you think you know, make parts of it happen. Focus on one thing at a time. It does not have to happen right away as everything has its own time. Stop using your clock. Don't use your projection on something that does not happen: a current reality. If you think something bad is going to happen, test it. See what happens."

Terri seemed confused.

"Cultural imperatives, for example: a female wanting to be the head of a big corporation. Test it. Trying is not a waste of time, whatever it is. The next thing is never say 'I can't' unless you don't want to accomplish your goal. Co-ordinate and start there."

"I am starting to see your point," Terri said. "The way I looked at becoming the CEO was to work hard, deliver the projects, do research and present brilliant ideas. I never gave up on my vision."

"I know the division into four parts may be a different perspective than traditional methods," I said. "I'm offering a way to reduce or eliminate the overwhelm of wanting that big thing. Most often overwhelm coupled with fear of failure causes most people to give up without taking any steps."

"It makes sense," Georgina added, and sipped her coffee. "I know I can be passionate about some great lofty ideas, but I wouldn't know where to start."

"I agree, but I'd really like to have an example of this division into four," Sarah said.

Nellie took another piece of dessert.

"What if you told us how you produced your big dance theater shows?" Mrs. Trevor asked me.

Everyone was amazed as they didn't know about this part of my life. I didn't really want to use it as an example, but they insisted.

"I had passion for dance, but it was culturally inappropriate to perform in public. After being trained for many years I decided to follow my dream while my real work was in finance and wealth management." I smiled.

They looked astonished.

"I wanted to showcase a dance theater production which I had no experience in, and no dance school to choose dancers from. But my passion was unstoppable."

Mrs. Trevor and Nellie looked mesmerized.

I counted the four parts on my hands.

1. I only had two dance stories in mind – not a complete show
2. I wanted artists and dancers who were passionate and loved to dance
3. I didn't think much about the cost although I had an approximate budget in mind
4. I envisioned dazzling costumes with haunting music

"Unbelievable!" Sarah exclaimed.

"I proceeded with my decision without having an official date for the show. Then under each category I divided the task into four more parts."

"Show us," Terri encouraged.

I counted the subsections on my hands again.

To look for passionate artists:

2a – I put ads in places to attract semi-professional artists who were extremely passionate

2b – I was willing to teach which I had never been interested in before

2c – When I interviewed professional artists I inquired about their passion and not so much for skills

2d – I observed and coordinated the passion of the artists with the passion of the show which had me as the starting point

"You have guts," Georgina said with appreciation.

I smiled.

Another section I divided into the four parts was the fact that I only had two dance pieces in mind.

2.i – I believed in the creative process; that I would be able to add dance numbers

2.ii – I allowed the passion of the artists to add to the overall story

2.iii – I took time to learn about producing dance theatre shows

2.iv – I allowed the passion of the show to dictate the next steps

"I commend you," said Mrs. Trevor.

I thanked her and felt so much joy and appreciation looking at their faces.

"On the way to that big thing we find satisfaction," I added. "This in turn ignites more passion or sustains our passion."

The maid brought us sherbets in different colors. She said they were homemade and to try them. We all took a different one and savored the flavors.

"The expectation of a spontaneous event has to change. It took a year before I was able to think about securing a date for our debut production," I continued. "By changing the event's clock if necessary and not feeling constant time pressure your passion is sustained and it allows for creativity."

"This is wonderful! I love this." Nellie walked to give me a big hug.

We ate the tasty sherbets and toasted to a passionate life.

"Another element is to realize that you have an effect and what you seek will happen faster." I raised my glass again. "Think how easily you may disregard that you have an effect, thinking you can't or it's too big. Obviously I didn't have any experience, but I forged ahead. My passion kindled the fire in everyone else in the group. If the effect isn't in opposition to you it is in co-operation with you. Don't force it with an absolute time. Change the nature of the event or change the time and you will achieve big things faster."

Sarah and Nellie were taking notes. Terri looked puzzled.

"Don't think of time as an absolute deadline," I addressed Terri. "Fear comes when you project that you have no effect." I continued: "Therefore for big things to happen faster don't pay attention to the smaller things that slow them down. Make the big thing smaller and timely and place an artificial deadline on the list. If it's important, it will be accomplished. If it's not, it won't."

Terri and Mrs. Trevor agreed. Georgina took another sip of her sherbet while I continued.

"Passion, time and the effect you have are key to making bigger things happen. Distractions are natural, so give yourself a reasonable timeframe. Pay attention to procrastination, not arbitrary timing.

"That is how I started and over time the productions got bigger and better."

All of a sudden the phone rang, and it startled me. I asked if I should continue and Mrs. Trevor nodded.

"Effective people allow themselves to be affected by their actions. You have to acknowledge your participation in whatever you do. Trust that you will have the big thing even if you don't know when! Take smaller steps and do your part. The rest takes care of itself. That's when magic comes in.

"Deny yourself the effect of fear; take the good effect of fear and exercise it."

"What do you mean?" Nellie asked.

"What is the purpose of the big thing?" I asked. "For example, is it to hear yourself play the piano or is it to move people when you play the piano?"

Georgina and Nellie pondered and looked at each other. Nellie asked me to continue.

"Passion and a sense of participation will allow you to accomplish the things you want to. You are not supposed to know how to make them happen! Just take the first step. Your fears don't matter, your actions do!

"We set up these supposed to's which only make it harder. You can only eat cereal through your mouth. There is no other way. How often do you try to figure out the how? Instead, think of what is important: the what.

64

"Think of it another way: you move a mountain one barrel at a time. But if you say 'I am building a mountain' you will exhaust your resources. To move a mountain you need to be halfway there already. Faster is a projection. You will only do something as much as it matters to you, in equal measure to the passion, time and importance you give it."

"What I'm hearing you say is that our perception and projection of what we're doing make it take longer or make us lose our sense of passion because we unnecessarily exhaust ourselves in the process?" Terri asked.

"Yes," I said, "because we are affected by our sense of what matters. The ability to know what matters and its relevance is key. The task will tell you what is important.

"We don't realize that failing does not add to our winning skills. Here is an example: Are you more afraid of not winning or of losing? Minimize the things you have no control over and maximize the things you do. Pay attention and don't make small things big. They will occupy all of your efforts and energy because they are determined to make the big things occur."

"I totally relate to what you're saying," Terri replied. "I sometimes pay attention to minute details that don't really matter in the bigger picture. I become myopic, and after spending so much time and energy I realize they weren't important."

"Of course, because that changes the purpose and intention," I added. "Change the things you have control over; look at what is required and do the smaller piece. With the smaller piece look at how relevant it is to the bigger picture and don't make it bigger than it needs to be to keep your passion alive."

"This is fascinating!" Sarah exclaimed.

I was delighted to see I had been able to break down the concept into chewable bites. "Make it smaller to make it possible; small enough to keep it successful and big enough to keep your passion. Big things are possible because they are not overly focused and not fueled by adrenaline. Adrenaline keeps you unfocused."

"You just want to get it done, right?" Georgina asked.

I nodded. "Adrenaline is released when we are excited. We don't pay attention to the little subtleties that make us successful. What is and what matters is what we care about. It is a relative impossibility to make the wrong decision. We always make the best possible choices based on all the things we believe, and they will always be the most beneficial. One best at a time, such that you can't make a better choice than the one you are making."

"I am beginning to see how this process worked for my husband building the company," Mrs. Trevor confirmed.

I added: "Think: if it is possible, do I really want this? Then your passion will want the big thing. In accomplishing something you realize you never had it before, and that is exciting. To increase joy and passion is to participate with passion and without pressure or performance."

Sparks enveloped the kitchen. We were all elated. We thanked Mrs. Trevor for the fabulous afternoon and departed after smelling the invigorating scent of the flowers one more time.

Chapter 4

Your Money

4

During the month after our last meeting, I called each member of our group to see if they wanted to talk about their passions and fears in the following session. Terri had commented that it would be a long process to overcome fears and break down all of the information I had shared, and Sarah suggested we move on. Everyone had a different issue they were dealing with during that time.

After lunch at Mrs. Trevor's beautiful home, in the city but surrounded by beautiful trees, ponds and pools, like a country resort, I thought it would be great to talk about money and finances. They all agreed.

I decided to have our gathering on a Saturday. I set up chairs in the gazebo and waited for their arrival.

We all sat down appreciating the cool breeze. I started the discussion by saying:

"I totally enjoyed our lunch at Mrs. Trevor's home."

They all nodded and smiled.

Mrs. Trevor said: "It was a pleasure, I enjoyed our gathering, as much as you did."

Sarah shook her head. "I still can't believe I was there. I had to pinch myself."

I smiled. "To reach our financial goals, it is important to write them down and draft a plan, a blueprint or a strategy to achieve our desired outcome. A financial plan consists of six elements:

1. Cash Flow & Budget
2. Net Worth Statement
3. Risk Management
4. Tax & Investment Planning
5. Retirement Planning
6. Wills & Estate."

I had sent them Your Financial Snapshot, and the women had filled out various worksheets before our meeting. Now they all eagerly pulled them out of their bags and purses.

We started with the Cash Flow & Budget. Recording detailed income and expenses is essential, whether you make $1,000 a month or $100,000 a month. And an up-to-date budget is necessary, as income and expenses may change.

We went through the budget form, starting with date and name at the top of the page.

"If you are married or living in common-law and combine your income and expenses," I began, "you can write both names. Those who do finances totally separate each need to have a separate form.

"Let's assume you are married," I said, "and you do your finances together. You write down your gross income and then your net income, which is your take home money after taxes and deductions. If you get paid every two weeks then you multiply your net pay by 26 and divide by 12 to get the correct monthly figure. Then add the two incomes: yours and your spouse's. If you are self-employed, depending on if you are a sole-proprietor or own a corporation, you would also write down your net take home personal income."

Georgina was wearing a beautiful colorful blouse. "My husband and I do our budget together."

I acknowledged. "Some of your expenses may be paid monthly, weekly, bi-weekly or annually. You must convert all expenses on a monthly or annual basis to be consistent.

"It is good to know your fixed expenses first, such as rent or mortgage, food, child care, car insurance and more. Then look at your discretionary expenses, such as entertainment, which includes dining out, going to concerts and shows, travel expenses and others. This way if you need to adjust your expenditures you know exactly how your money is spent and can make the necessary changes."

I gave them a list of sample expenditures, such as mortgage or rent, utilities, insurance, car repair or maintenance, plus food, gifts, hobbies, clothing and travel.

As they scribbled away and sipped on iced tea, I reminded them that one-time purchases are categorized differently, such as a new car or new furniture, as these are not ongoing expenses unless they are financed.

"It is also important to distinguish between fixed and discretionary expenses so you can control your budget. If your income is limited and your goals are especially important to you within the timeframe that you have indicated, then you make a decision whether to spend your money on these items or not."

"Oh my goodness, I didn't realize how much I spend on discretionary expenses," Terri voiced.

"Well, you are enjoying your life. You obviously save and invest enough, right?" I asked.

She wiggled her shoulders as if to say she wasn't sure.

I suggested it might be easier to write down expenses in the following manner: fixed expenses on the left and discretionary expenses on the right, to see what results.

Sarah sighed and said she could hardly cover her fixed expenses.

"It's crucial to learn about cash flow because it keeps you focused on your goals and spending habits. If you overspend or your income is not what you desire, you can look for ways to increase your income. All various income and expense sources are listed on Your Financial Snapshot.

"Then you can look at questions such as if you are a sole proprietor what salary do you pay yourself? If you own a business and are a shareholder in the company do you take a salary or dividends? You will need to take the actual personal income that you receive from the company and use it as your personal income and not mix it up with the company budget. You subtract your expenses from your income. If the result is a positive number that is your uncommitted income. It can reveal opportunities to save and invest on a regular basis so you can reach your financial goals. If it is negative you are in trouble; a major change is necessary."

"You can say that again," Sarah fretted.

Everyone looked either puzzled or irritated except Mrs. Trevor, who was listening patiently.

"I guess I wanna be able to afford my rent, go out once in a while, and have money for my kid," Sarah continued.

"I have no idea about budgets. My husband pays for everything." Nellie's forehead creased with worry.

"What happens if God forbid he died?" Terri asked.

"I am sure there will be enough money for me. He says, 'I will always take care of you'," Nellie shot back.

Mrs. Trevor looked around the circle of women, stopping at Sarah, and began to reminisce. "I remember my husband was making ten dollars a week and we used to save one dollar every week. I tell you at times it was extremely difficult. That dollar could have come in handy."

"How come you saved if you didn't have enough?" Sarah asked.

Mrs. Trevor continued: "We always saved ten percent for a rainy day, and it paid off. You cannot spend more money than what you make, but what you can do is decide what is important to you. This way you are happy to allocate your funds to achieve your goals."

"Looking at the numbers in black and white is making me think," Terri said. "Is buying a designer purse important? I wonder if I do it to protect my self-image? Or simply to enjoy the luxury? Can I do without it?"

Nellie smiled. "I like designer purses."

"Who doesn't?" Sarah growled.

"I never really paid attention to money issues before," Nellie confessed.

"Welcome to the real world," Georgina said.

"I am really thankful to be here," Nellie replied.

"You know," Mrs. Trevor began, "some of the friends I grew up with are on government support. They cannot survive without it. They didn't spend their money wisely."

"I sure don't wanna be like that when I'm old and gray," Sarah blurted.

"My mother relied on the government for support," Georgina offered.

Sarah looked at her. "Did she ever work?"

"For a short time. Her only source of income was the government. Those days women didn't work much, and my father didn't make a lot of money either."

This was the perfect time to introduce my next point.

"We all have choices in life; they made their choices and lived accordingly. Even a small amount like $50 a week savings at 8% return will be more than $280,000 in 30 years. And savings need to start no matter the amount of our earnings. I remember many years ago someone told me if he only made $2,500 a month he would be happy. Then after making it he said if he just made another $1,000 a month he'd be happy. He said he kept making more money as he strived for more, but he also kept spending more and was never able to save."

I felt enthusiastic about how open they were to the subject.

"Affirmations are one way to get your mind to focus on your desired outcome. Your thoughts have the power to manifest. If you use affirmations on a daily basis, you will notice a shift in your way of thinking, and this could open up a new world of possibilities. You must believe it can work and most importantly you must take action."

As I listed some affirmations, the women gratefully wrote them down:

- My income now far exceeds my expenses.
- Every dollar I spend comes back to me multifold.
- I now have more money than I need.
- The money I make helps society for the good of all concerned.
- I deserve to have as much money as I want.
- The universe is abundant, and it supports me in my wealth accumulation.
- Money comes to me easily and I can freely spend it if I wish to.

"The question becomes," I continued, "can you actually see yourself owning a lot of money and wealth in your life? It's essential to realize that if in the past you have done what you could do based on your abilities and circumstances, then what will you do differently now for your future?"

Mrs. Trevor adjusted her glasses. "My experience was similar, although I didn't use any affirmations. I just didn't entertain negative thoughts such as 'we are not going to be able to put the children to school, or we can't afford to buy a house.' I always believed we were going to be comfortable."

Sarah shook her head in wonder. "It's still beyond me to think like that when I don't have any money."

"The idea here is to be hopeful that you can do something about it and not give into your fears, because we all have them," Terri explained. Sarah pursed her lips.

Georgina was quiet as always, deep in her thoughts.

After a brief break to move our bodies a little and breathe to refresh our brains, I asked: "Do you all know what your net worth is?"

"I do," Mrs. Trevor replied quickly.

"You mean how much money I have?" Sarah asked.

"What's that?" Nellie wanted to know. "You mean how much we are worth?"

Georgina nodded.

"Yes," I said. "Net worth is all your assets minus all your liabilities."

"Zero , a big fat zero!" Sarah shouted.

Everyone's body language revealed their anxiety. Except Mrs. Trevor.

"Relax," she said. "It's only money. You are not going to take it with you."

"You can always leave it to me if it's extra," Sarah smiled.

Mrs. Trevor gave Sarah a blank look.

I explained that there are three types of assets:

1. Cash Assets, which is money in liquid form such as savings or checking accounts, government bonds, money market funds.

2. Investment Assets, which include investments such as Registered Retirement Savings Plans (RRSP), Registered Retirement Income Funds (RRIF), 401Ks, individual retirement accounts (IRA), stocks, bonds, Guaranteed Investment Certificates, Tax Free Savings Accounts (TFSA), mutual funds, Exchange-traded funds (ETF), rental properties, businesses, pension plans (commuted values), cottage or vacation properties.

3. Personal Assets, which include principal residence, automobile, boat, trailer, motor bike, antiques, stamp or art collections, personal belongings like televisions, computers at market value.

"The sum of all these main three categories are Total Assets," I said. "Then we have Liabilities."

I outlined that liabilities are categorized as short term and long term. Short term includes credit card debts, personal loans such as a car loan or family loan, lines of credit and taxes payable. Long term includes mortgages and loans longer than ten years.

"Here's a tip for you," I added. "It would be a good idea to consolidate all your short term debts into one and get the best interest rate possible from your lending institution."

Terri and Mrs. Trevor agreed with my point as I continued my explanation:

"The sum total of those short and long term items are your Total Liabilities. Net Worth which is the second element in a financial plan is your total assets less your total liabilities. Your Net Worth Statement is at a specific moment in time, and it changes as your assets or liabilities change."

Sarah looked worried. "My worth is zero, actually less than zero, nada. I'm in debt. I'm worth nothing."

"Sarah, I want you to know that your worth as a human being is not based on your financial worth," I soothed.

She looked at me with disbelief.

I continued while looking her in the eye. "Some people don't have much to show financially and yet have a lot of ideas, creativity, passion, ambition, and purpose."

"I don't know our net worth. I am sure we own millions of dollars," Nellie claimed.

Georgina chuckled: "I'd guess we are a quarter millionaire."

Mrs. Trevor burst out laughing. "Currently I am worth more than I can count."

"How about you, Terri?" I asked.

"Actually I am disappointed. I don't have as much as I thought I had and would like to have."

I lay my arm on Terri's shoulder.

Sarah started pacing. "Forget about all this. I wanna be worth something. I'm worth nothing!" she exclaimed with sadness in her eyes.

This is not just about money, I thought, and warmly offered: "Honey, you are worth a lot. Just because you're not in a favorable financial position right now, it does not mean you aren't worth anything. Your worth as a person has nothing to do with money. You are a unique individual. You are as important on this earth as anybody else."

She stopped pacing and returned to her seat.

"You matter! You can slowly start saving and build. You are young and have time ahead of you."

Sarah looked at me with a glimmer of hope.

"An important point to remember is to have emergency reserves in case of a disastrous situation. Your financial plan must have provisions for either a few months of expenses or at least line of credit available prior to experiencing financial hardship. The best time to apply for credit is when you have income and assets. Generally the higher your income the more credit you will be able to get approved for if your credit score is good.

"It's paramount especially for women to become familiar with their finances instead of always having their husband or partner take care of it. Often women endure difficult experiences and miss opportunities to advance themselves due to a lack of knowledge or a relationship breakdown. Nellie, could you ask your husband for a statement of assets and liabilities? Also find out if all the assets are jointly in your names or his name alone?"

Her face grew red. "I'm not sure if he will, and what do you mean his name only?" She paused and then continued. "I know I signed some papers for the business but I have no idea what it is worth. How do I find out?"

"Every business produces a financial report called a Balance Sheet, similar to the Net Worth Statement we are talking about. Business owners often know the value; otherwise it can be appraised by a professional."

I said: "In order to reach your financial goals you must know your net worth. However, if you are provided for, it would be wise to become familiar with your partner's finances and possibly become involved in the financial discussions.

"Usually I would start with short, medium and long -term goals, but today I wanted to start the conversation with Cash Flow and Net Worth Statement. Sarah, you indicated you'd like to be rich. What is rich to you?"

"Dunno, have loads of money," she said.

"How much is loads?" I asked.

She paused. "What I really want is to be comfortable."

I knew people have different comfort levels, but before I asked what comfortable meant to Sarah, Terri yelled: "Not in million years are you gonna have money, Sarah, with the way you're thinking!"

Tension was building. Sarah gave Terri a dirty look and stopped herself from saying something she might regret.

"I got promoted to CEO last year and make high six figures with stock options. I am inspired to do more and invest in my future," Terri shared.

"You are a strong woman, Terri. Keep it up," Mrs. Trevor advised.

Terri smiled in appreciation of the comment.

I continued: "Often individuals with higher net worth are risk takers. Risk takers want to earn as much as they can and are willing to go through the ups and downs for higher earnings. They open businesses and are quite entrepreneurial. The other category are security oriented and they need to have a secure, steady income, although nothing in life is secure. Risk takers have increased potential for earnings and asset accumulation. They have more opportunities to increase income and attract more money. However their spending habits may be large as well so they don't necessarily build wealth.

"In addition, wealthy people tend to make regular donations. When you give without worry or feeling a lack of money, you will attract more money. It is one of the most fundamental principles of the Universe. When you give with love and joy, and no attachments, you will receive multifold."

"My husband and I always gave as much as we could to our church. I still do," Mrs. Trevor added.

"I am not religious. I'm not even sure if God exists," Sarah said.

"I don't like to give to church. Well, if I feel like it. Once a year I give to my favorite organization," Georgina said.

Terri sat straight in her seat. "I have mixed feelings about this. Just because one does not give, does not mean they cannot have a lot of money." She paused and added: "I am sensitive about animal abuse, so I give to different organizations. I donate generously on a regular basis."

Everyone murmured in agreement.

"True," I said. "I'm merely bringing the habits of the rich to your attention.

"The psychology of money is interesting. It is often after doing a budget and a net worth statement that you become aware of what you truly desire when it comes to wealth. I'd like to spend a few minutes on this subject."

They all expressed curiosity.

"It can take time for thoughts about money to travel from our mind and psyche and return in the form of a physical or mental manifestation. If we want to manifest something, we've got to think about the subject with concentrated focus and real desire. In some cases, the manifestation can happen instantly and other times it may take years.

"If you try hard and make a lot of effort but it doesn't work no matter what you do, then you may have subconscious beliefs that are in opposition to your conscious mind. You may have subconscious thoughts such as: 'I am not worthy of wealth' or 'My family is poor, what makes me different? Of course I'll end up like them.' Or 'I don't deserve success.'. If these are the thoughts you entertain, you will not be able to manifest your desires as quickly because your mind may be confused."

Nellie and Georgina gave me inquisitive looks and Mrs. Trevor poured herself some more iced tea.

"On the one hand, you want wealth and success, but your subconscious has an opposing thought like I don't deserve it." I continued: "It's like you're in a taxi cab and you tell the driver to go north, then after a few minutes you say, no go south. The driver will be confused and, by going north and then south you will see you are stagnant. You will find yourself at the same spot you started."

Sarah stood up and crossed her arms.

"The point is to realize your hidden and subconscious thoughts, because unless you deal with them you cannot move forward easily," I added.

"At the start of our discussion we talked about our goals. A useful exercise now would be to take a piece of paper and write My Ideal Situation at the top. Draw a horizontal line right below that and another vertical line in the middle of the page. Write a goal on the left side and wait for a response or a feeling. Don't force it. When your response comes, write the exact message on the right side. Continue writing your goals one at a time on the left hand side and wait for your response then write it on the right side.

Sarah and Georgina volunteered to name a few.

MY SITUATION

I want to have $100,000	Who do you think you are? Mom & Dad never had that kind of money.
I like to have a secure & comfortable future	Well the only security I can think of is food and shelter. Forget about comfort.
I want to get rid of my debt	Are you joking? Life is so hard. Everybody I know has debt. I will never be able to be debt free.

"It's interesting," I said, "once you write a goal or a situation, you will notice that your response comes almost automatically. In rare cases it might take a while, but generally you will find that you always have an answer. Now, after you finish your goal list, go back to the right side and write a new statement. This reinforces your mind to think in a new way."

I offered an example.

MY IDEAL SITUATION

I want to have $100,000	*I deserve to have money. I am not my parents. I am a unique individual.*
I like to have a secure & comfortable future	*My past does not represent my future. I am mentally and financially working on my goal and I will make every effort to ensure a comfortable future.*
I want to get rid of my debt	*I am already working on paying off my debt and I am extremely excited about that. I have a plan and I fully intend to achieve my goal.*

I looked at the group. "Over time you will notice a change in attitude. When you start reprogramming your mind in a new way, new neuropathways open up and gradually replace the old programming.

"You may have positive responses during this exercise and if so, that's great. One of my favorite phrases is: I attract money like a magnet."

Georgina cheered: "Very interesting exercises."

"They are, aren't they?" Terri said with excitement. "I must admit that even though I didn't think about thoughts the way you explained, now that I analyze it, I've always had positive responses and thoughts that I can do what I intend. I can use this exercise to increase my wealth beyond my comfort level and see what comes up."

I smiled back. "Wonderful. Now, would you all like to take a break and have some refreshments?" I asked.

We chatted and enjoyed the beautiful air in the backyard. All that hard work had made us hungry, so we ordered food. Terri said she had become a vegetarian in the last few years and Mrs. Trevor said she did not eat pork, frogs or octopus. "I don't care for delicatessen," as she put it. But she loved Chinese food, and that suited all of us so that's what we ordered. We had fun.

Two and a half weeks passed. It was a rainy day, one of those days where you felt you just want to cuddle in bed and forget everything. We all sat in my living room. Georgina was not her usual sweet, friendly self. She was stirring the sugar in her tea cup so fast and loud it disturbed everyone.

"You know," she said, "it's all her fault. My sister-in-law, she has to meddle with everything, and the worst part is my husband listens to her. I don't know what's going on." She slapped her thigh.

"Oh I could tell you stories about my brother-in-law," Nellie agreed. "All the grief he caused us about money."

"You should be happy you've got family. I don't want to hear about it," Terri said. Georgina screamed: "Just shut up! What do you know about anything in life, besides money and success? You are so self-absorbed; you can't see anything else."

Terri snapped: "Excuse me, what are you talking about?"

Mrs. Trevor murmured: "I am not feeling well."

"Just be quiet for a minute," Georgina yelled.

Mrs. Trevor gave her an unkind look.

"Georgina, what's the matter? Why are you upset?" I asked.

She started crying.

Although Sarah had seemed enthusiastic when she arrived, she didn't know how to handle this and left the room to get a glass of water.

"My husband had a lover on the side all this time. Bastard. I thought he loved me. We have two beautiful children. What's going to happen now?"

"I am so sorry." Terri leaned to one side. "I have a friend who is an excellent lawyer. You can take your husband to the cleaners."

Georgina sobbed. "I can't divorce him! I don't make enough money. What about the kids?" She continued crying. "And I love him."

Mrs. Trevor was not well at all. She wanted to lie down. So we decided to take a few minutes to ourselves until everyone calmed down. I went to the kitchen to make chamomile tea and Nellie followed me. She told me she felt confused by all the different discussions we'd had, as if her reality or perception of life had been challenged. I assured her it was temporary and to embrace her feelings. She suggested we all do some light yoga exercises together to get centered. Mrs. Trevor relaxed on the living room couch while we went to the studio in the basement to stretch.

Twenty minutes later we came back to the kitchen and drank some tea. Mrs. Trevor had taken a power nap, and everyone was feeling better. I wanted to discuss the third element in a financial plan, Risk Management, but it didn't seem timely.

Georgina told us how upset she was, and how she felt betrayed about her husband having an affair with another woman. She wondered if she should file for divorce. Georgina asked about the legal ramifications and the best options possible.

Everybody showed compassion and sincere concern for Georgina.

Mrs. Trevor cleared her throat. "Georgina, you are a strong, beautiful woman. Sometimes marriage needs a bit of work. I have two questions for you. One, how long has he been seeing this other woman? And two, does your husband love you?"

"I hate men," Sarah spat.

"Isn't that a bit harsh?" Nellie asked.

Sarah gave her a mean look in reply.

Georgina said: "I confronted my husband about it. He denied it at first, but then admitted it. He said it has been three years. He said that he loved me, and she meant nothing to him. I'm not sure what to think."

"If he says he loves you, you have to believe him. If he didn't he would leave you." Nellie pouted her lips.

"Not necessarily," Terri said. "He has to pay support. This way he has his cake and eats it too."

"Bastard!" Sarah yelled.

"Sarah, you're still angry. What's going on?" Mrs. Trevor asked.

Sarah stood up. "All men want is sex."

"Georgina, if you want to divorce him you have to stay separated for a while before the court will grant you a divorce," I said. "My question to you is, are you prepared to make a separation agreement?"

"I don't know, I don't know," she replied with tears in her eyes.

Nellie asked: "Do you have a marriage contract or a prenuptial agreement?"

"What's the difference?" Georgina wondered.

"No difference," Terri said. "It means the same thing. How about you, Nellie?"

"Absolutely not," Nellie responded. "My husband wanted one and I said, if you don't trust me I'm not going to marry you, so he dropped the subject."

"Lucky you. I guess he loved you a lot," Sarah said.

"He still does," Nellie happily sang.

Georgina went on: "No, we don't have anything written down. My husband did not have much when we got married."

"If you built everything together, you will be entitled to half of the net assets," I explained. "In a marriage contract which is drafted and signed before marriage, you document your net worth at the time, and assets brought into the marriage, make provisions for division of property, spousal support and child support, and other issues in case of a marriage breakdown."

"We didn't really have anything except he inherited a small sum of money when his father died. We added it to our savings for a down payment on our house," Georgina said.

She began asking different financial questions, but instead I asked her: "The question is, can you handle living on your own and taking care of the children if you get custody and possibly spousal and child support? Are you ready for that big undertaking?"

Mrs. Trevor took a deep breath. "Children are a big responsibility, Georgina. They need constant care, and they need their father around."

Georgina cried quietly.

A couple of tears ran down Sarah's cheeks. "You know my daughter Anusha is only two and a half years old, but she acts like she's seven. She keeps asking where Daddy is. I can't tell her he left, so I keep saying he'll come soon."

"I had a friend whose boyfriend left her as soon as he found out she was pregnant, so when the baby was born, she decided to say his daddy was dead," Terri said.

"I guess everyone handles it as best as they can," Nellie added.

Georgina leaned back on the couch: "I think women just want to be heard and understood."

"True, my dear. And we like to associate with people we care about," said Mrs. Trevor.

"I would say trust is the most important. I'm not sure if I trust anyone," Sarah claimed.

"Expressing our feelings is crucial if we are to have open communication," I added.

Strangely, a few phone calls came in at the same time. We burst out laughing because our cells were always on silent mode. We took a few minutes break and reconvened in the living room.

"We have discussed having short term and long term financial goals. We have also discussed Cash Flow and Net Worth Statements. The third element in a financial plan is Risk Management, which includes all types of insurance.

"I have discovered an interesting concept: some people have the sense they will live to a certain age."

"I've heard that too. Is it true?" Georgina asked.

"I believe it to be true, but an approximate age, not an exact age, and provided you have a sense of knowing as opposed to thinking about it."

Nellie played with her wedding ring. "I can see an element of truth to that."

" Let's take a moment and share what age you believe you will live to," I said.

"Maybe another four, five years," Mrs. Trevor said.

Terri followed Mrs. Trevor: "I have absolutely no idea."

"I don't want to think about it," Georgina worried. "What will happen to my boys?"

Nellie said: "I think I will live to around 75; that's enough."

Everyone looked surprised.

Sarah seemed agitated. "I'm still processing what this means. Maybe I can tell you later."

"Imagine you could live five to ten years longer than the age you thought. How would you feel? Are you taking steps to live a healthy life? To be more involved in life, to participate fully and be totally engaged increases the joy we feel. This releases the joy hormone or oxytocin, which in turn increases happiness. The more you live life, the slower you age. The more you participate with life, the less you age," I continued.

"Anyway, what's the point of life?" Georgina whispered. "It seems like the rug has been pulled out from under my feet. I thought my husband and I were tight. I trusted him, but now it's like nothing matters anymore."

"Whether you are married or not, or whether you are with someone or not doesn't really matter. I wonder who I am building wealth for," Terri complained.

"Hope," Sarah encouraged.

"Pardon me?" Terri was surprised.

"You know, hope, that maybe, just maybe things will work out." Sarah spoke with a hopeful voice.

"I am glad to hear you say that, Sarah." Mrs. Trevor patted her on the shoulder.

Georgina yearned: "My only hope is my two boys. As far as my husband is concerned, he can rot in hell."

"Talk about rotting in hell, does he have life insurance?" Terri asked.

"Terri, aren't you being a bit insensitive today?" Mrs. Trevor frowned.

"Well I don't know," Georgina responded, "but we took some insurance in case we died, mostly for the kids."

I explained the importance of life insurance for a variety of reasons.

"One main reason is to provide for your children and support your loved ones in case of death. Depending on whether the need for support is temporary or not, you may choose from two basic kinds of life insurance policies: term insurance and permanent insurance. Term insurance has no savings component, and it is for a certain term. If there is no claim, there is no payout during the term."

"So you are saying that I can get insurance like that for myself?" Sarah asked.

"Yes, life insurance policies are taken for the benefit of others, called beneficiaries. In case of death, dependents who rely on your financial support will benefit."

"How much insurance should I have?" she asked.

I told her enough to provide for food, shelter, clothing, schooling and more until her child was at least eighteen years old.

Mrs. Trevor said: "I believe I have some kind of insurance that pays dividends."

"Your kids are grown up. Why do you need insurance?" Sarah asked.

"To cover taxes on death," she responded.

"My husband said he took out insurance so when he died the business would continue without interruption. Even though I lived a wealthy life, I didn`t want to hear about it. When Gabby died a few years ago I was affected intensely. Not only the deep pain of losing my husband but the day to day financial management became over-whelming. Despite being involved with the company finances, if my eldest son hadn't been running the company, I would have been lost. I owned half the company and was the sole beneficiary of my husband's estate. That said, we had a lot of different agreements in place for the company. I couldn't really focus on any finances. I was married to Gabby almost all of my life and I had a hard time dealing with everything."

"Understandable," I added. "If you depend on your spouse or another person for support the first thing to remember is that you need to take charge of the situation. You can find out if you would be eligible to receive any income from the deceased in the form of pension income, life insurance or simply government support. Be proactive."

Nellie expressed concern. "I would be in total chaos if my husband died."

"At times like that the mind and emotions can get cloudy and interpret financial and emotional loss as one big challenge. If your financial security is threatened you might fall into the fear mode and feel paralyzed. When in fear, run the numbers logically and ask the questions, think about possible outcomes and make your decision.

"The idea here is to take steps, even if they are baby steps, and look for solutions. It's easy to feel sorry for yourself, like a victim of circumstance, but courage and determination will go a long way. You've got to put your fears in perspective," I added.

Mrs. Trevor turned to Nellie. "I suggest you start familiarizing yourself with finances, however big or small, and find out how your husband runs his company."

Nellie nodded with confidence.

"Other types of insurance under Risk Management are disability, critical illness and long term care insurance." I listed them on the whiteboard. "Change is the only thing that is constant in life, and that can be frightening. As human beings we don't like change because we don't want the unknown. What may prompt us to change are hope and courage.

"One of our greatest potentials is the ability to earn money. If we're working and making money, chances are we want and need money; otherwise we would do volunteer work without pay. If you cannot work, will you be able to pay your bills and ensure a solid future?" I asked.

There were some deep sighs.

"Some unexpected life changing events might be: loss of health which may impact your income; loss of your job or your business; or death of your income earning partner or family member. The important factor is to ensure your finances are not drained and are properly protected in case of illness or injury. If employed, you may have disability insurance at work, and it may have certain clauses and restrictions in order to qualify. Though there may be some form of government assistance, the amount and the duration of pay may not be sufficient. It's always advisable to know what you need financially, and what is available to you."

Nellie kept moving in her seat.

Sarah shot Nellie a sarcastic look. "What's the matter Nellie? You wouldn't know anything about this, right? With your rich husband. Most of us have to work."

Sarah, you made your choice, she made hers," Terri jumped in.

"I didn't choose to get pregnant and have the guy leave me without a word," Sarah threw back.

"Maybe getting pregnant was good. You have an angel on your side," Mrs. Trevor comforted her.

"God knows how much I love Anusha, but you know how hard it is to make a living? What if I get sick or get hurt?" Sarah choked up.

"Do you know how hard it is to even make it through the day? I have absolutely no help, emotionally or financially. My parents don't even want to talk to me."

"Why is that?" Terri asked.

Sarah inhaled deeply. "They never liked my boyfriend when we were dating. Maybe they were right, 'cause when he found out I was pregnant he just left. My parents shouldn't have brushed me off though. I admit I was wild. I smoked, I partied, and they were always on my case. So anyways, when Anusha's dad left, I decided to keep her. I felt a big bond right from the beginning with her in my belly. My parents thought I was crazy. They spoke to me about giving her up for adoption. They kept telling me I was a kid myself. I couldn't possibly do anything right." She paused. "They said I'd never amount to anything."

"That's very unfortunate, my dear. Parents always want the best for their children, but if children don't act according to their expectations, sometimes parents don't handle the situation properly," Mrs. Trevor pointed out.

"Well anyways that's the past." Sarah responded and looked at me. "You were talking about some insurance."

"If you are unable to work, how would you pay your bills? Maybe through savings, investments, family help, or perhaps borrow money.

But how long would that last?" I asked.

"If my husband can't work I wouldn't want him to sell his business. I need to know more about this." Nellie sounded distressed.

I wrote on the board the three main questions to ask when getting a disability policy:

1. How much would I get paid through the policy?
2. How long would I get paid for?
3. When would the payments start?

"If you own a business, the company can buy insurance for the owners or the key employees," I added.

Nellie pointed out the insurance section of the Financial Snapshot I had given them, and she said she would look into it.

"Any chance of reconciling with your husband?" I asked Georgina. "You really need to get your finances in order."

She said no.

"When we get older it's harder to look after ourselves," said Mrs. Trevor.

I agreed and continued. "While disability insurance pays if you are unable to perform your duties at work due to injury or illness, long term care insurance pays a monthly tax free amount if you are unable to do any two of the following six activities by yourself."

I again wrote them on the board:

1. Eating
2. Bathing
3. Moving to or from a chair or bed
4. Toileting

5. Continence
6. Dressing

Nellie seemed to be worried. I suggested she have a conversation with her husband.

"Critical illness is another form of insurance which pays a tax free lump sum to the insured in case of a major illness like cancer or a heart attack."

"My daughter Sonia had bought this insurance. When she became ill with cancer the insurance company paid out which was helpful," Mrs. Trevor shared with grief in her eyes.

"I have both critical illness and disability insurance. I am terrified of becoming sick," Terri said.

Nellie expressed: "Maybe I should get that in case I get sick."

"So your husband might not stick around if you are too old or too sick?" Sarah asked sarcastically.

Nellie looked terrified.

Mrs. Trevor told her to relax. "Don't doubt your husband's love. Do you have a reason to believe he doesn't love you?"

"No!" Nellie replied confidently.

Mrs. Trevor spread her hands to make the point.

"There are of course other types of insurance like hospital plans, accident insurance and many more," I advised. "In addition there is insurance for your automobile, home, boat and other items such as your collectibles. All of this is under the Risk Management section. If you are a professional it's important to have liability insurance and business insurance is another one to keep in mind if you own one. It's best to seek advice from your financial planners, lawyers and accountants."

We had covered a lot. They all showed interest in completing the Financial Snapshot I had provided. It was late, so we said good night to reconvene another day.

A month passed. Nellie told us she was enchanted by our money discussions. She invited us to her husband's company for our next meeting. When we all arrived, the receptionist informed Nellie and her husband. They came to reception and welcomed us. Nellie introduced her husband who was a tall, handsome, sophisticated looking man. He greeted us warmly and invited us to sit in the board room. It felt great.

Sarah looked inspired and was smiling like a little child in a candy store. She said: "I'm getting used to this high life."

Georgina was quiet. Mrs. Trevor looked a little weak.

We sat in the board room. I was passionate to talk about the fourth element of a financial plan, Tax & Investment Planning. I thought I would discuss Investment Planning that day and cover Taxation on a different day.

I wanted to start with investments, but everyone was at a different level both in knowledge and wealth ownership. The important point was to distinguish investing from saving, so I began the conversation.

"Money in your bank account or cash on hand is merely savings. Once you save, the money starts growing and it can be a wonderful thing. Saving for an item such as a car or a house or for emergencies is very different than investing for the future.

"As discussed earlier, it takes discipline to save or even invest. Are you a natural saver or a spender?" I asked.

Nellie said: "I enjoy shopping. It feels good to spend money."

Terri said she had become more of a saver.

"It's good to save ten percent of your earnings every year for a start. Savings can be accumulated in a variety of ways such as a bank account, a money market fund, or government treasury bills," I continued. "Investing is even more important. If you saved $5,000 a year at 10% rate of return, in 20 years you will have $315,000.

"Investments may be in stocks, government or corporate bonds, ETF's, mutual funds real estate, foreign currencies, businesses, private equity and more.

"To decide how to invest our money, we often use the Rule of 72. In order to double your money you divide 72 by the number of years in which you wish to double your money. That gives the rate of return you must receive in order to achieve that. For example if you want to double your money in 10 years you will need a return of 7.2% (72 ◎10) and if you would like to double your money in 5 years, you will need a rate of return of 14.2% (72 ◎ 5)."

Nellie smiled. "Interesting," she said.

"To emphasize the power of compounding a lump sum investment of $100,000 at 8% in nine years will generate almost $200,000. by adding regularly to your investments, your earnings will increase over time. In this example if you add $500 a month to your investments in nine years, you will own almost $275,000," I said joyfully.

"One of the main reasons most people are unable to invest is because they overspend and get into debt. The invention of credit cards has been useful to many people, but it has also been a source of pain and hardship for others. The use of credit cards is advantageous when travelling, or perhaps accumulating points. Generally, it is three to four weeks from the time of purchase to the time of payment, therefore if credit is used properly the amount of money spent in that period could be used for something else until payment is due. Caution must be used not to leave a balance on the credit card because the interest charged is quite high and usually not tax deductible.

"A line of credit is another way to borrow money without any set payments or time constraints. For example, a $10,000 line of credit can give you access to money if needed urgently generally at a lower rate than credit card rates. You can use the funds on the line of credit and pay all or part of the funds back, in a very short period of time and only pay interest based on the days used. This is a rotating credit."

Sarah and Georgina were taking notes. The board room had a large, oval mahogany table with twelve comfortable black chairs that rocked. Mrs. Trevor sat at the head of the table. She was comfortable in that position and leaned in as if to teach us a lesson.

"I am old school; if you don`t have money to spend, wait until you do. The only time we borrowed money was when we bought our house. We took a mortgage from the bank at a very low rate. The other time we borrowed money was when my husband and I started our company. Of course the interest was tax deductible."

I was sitting at the other end of the table. Terri was on my right. As a CEO she felt at ease in the board room. She stood up and walked behind me, to a whiteboard. I rolled my chair to the left and indicated for her to go ahead.

"We live in a society where we want everything and are not willing to wait," Terri began, "therefore we easily spend money we don't have in order to get the things we want." She paused briefly.

"Do you know how we as women get rid of depression or upset? Well you guessed right; shopping, oh yes, shopping. It feels good. Why? Because we put on new clothes, makeup, shoes, and we look good and we feel good. It makes us happy, or even better we buy gifts for the ones we love. We may buy books or programs to get fresh, new ideas. Of course, some might buy more food and more food, since eating changes our emotion. Normally that feels better in the beginning but then we keep complaining about the weight or the money we don't have. Well as women we feel different every day and we can change our minds at any time."

Mrs. Trevor leaned back in her chair, tilted her head and asked: "You, Terri?"

"Oh yes," she responded. "As disciplined as I was, I would go on shopping sprees, especially when I felt challenged at work or would have difficulty in my relationships." She paced back and forth. "The bottom line is we want to feel good and be happy. If we spend more than we can afford, we are trying to put a band-aid on our pains and relationship problems."

Everyone seemed surprised and yet agreed with what she said. She continued. "Personally, I love the high life but I have no attachments to money. To me money comes easily and for years unfortunately money went easily as well. I always lived exactly how I wanted, spent as much as I wanted. At some point I started saving and investing. That was going well for a while, but guess what? I would cash it in, spend it and start all over again. I did not have a plan. I started working when I was sixteen and I am thirty-eight now. I started paying attention to my finances, hired professionals and became disciplined only seven years ago."

As she took her seat, everyone clapped at how humble, loveable and vulnerable Terri had just shown herself to be.

For the first time Sarah's eyes sparked as if there was hope.

Georgina was in deep thought. "I think my husband and I are a little disciplined. We save some money."

I rolled my chair back in. "In order to be disciplined you need to take steps to be in control. Coming from a place of choice is empowering. You can consciously choose not to overspend by recognizing your actions and replacing the habit with something more positive, then rewarding yourself for it. This is why budgeting is crucial. Don't overthink it if you don't follow through occasionally, as long as the impulse spending is not a pattern. With proper budgeting you will be able to allocate money to things that really matter to you. It may be hard at first but with practice and increased awareness you can do it."

"And," Mrs. Trevor added, "I know people who will not spend money on anything unless they have to, because they feel they don't deserve the pleasure of new things or abundance, like new clothing, furniture, travel and so forth. And some feel guilty spending money."

I agreed and shared my view that if your desired lifestyle does not match your income, you have some choices:

1. Change your lifestyle to meet your income
2. Change your income to match your lifestyle

"Well said, my dear," Mrs. Trevor cheered.

"Thank you, Mrs. Trevor," I replied. I looked around the room. "Prosperity Consciousness versus Poverty Consciousness is a concept I find interesting. Some people are naturally Wealth Conscious. Wealth Consciousness is living in abundance. Although the word wealth is associated with money I define Wealth Conscious as when you live a wealthy, joyous life. Wealthy in this context is when you enjoy your wealth whatever amount you happen to own, and you are generous with it."

Everyone was intrigued. I gave them the Wealth Consciousness quiz to discover their consciousness.

I stood up and continued. "Once you are ready to invest, you must know how much risk you can take and the fluctuations you can tolerate in your investments. You each have different risk tolerance levels therefore to invest wisely you must know your Risk Profile."

I listed the necessary questions on the board and advised them to think before investing:

1. What is your willingness level to take investment risks?
2. What is your expected rate of return either in percentage or dollars?
3. Investments can go up or down in value over a particular period of time. How much could the total value of all of your investments drop before you feel uncomfortable?
4. How would you describe your investment style?

Georgina sighed. "A lot to think about."

I handed them each the Risk Profile questionnaire.

"Another important element to consider when investing is your time horizon. Are the investments for a short or long term? For example, are the investments for your retirement or your children's education? Or are they for your dream vacation in a couple of years, buying a home or leaving a legacy for your family?

"A variety of investment options are available, including local or global investments; they may be in specific geographic areas like Canada, the USA, Europe, China, India or South Africa. Or they can be in a specific industry like technology, pharmaceuticals, bank stocks or government bonds. It may also be in real estate, or company mergers and acquisitions. Risk factors can include economic risk, political risk or currency risk."

Nellie was jubilant. "Captivating."

I giggled with happiness seeing the women taking an interest in finances.

"Your investment objectives, your time horizon and your risk profile are crucial elements in determining your investment options and strategies to achieve your desired outcome. You need to find your risk profile to determine if you are a conservative investor, an aggressive investor or in between.

"Sometimes you may look for a fast, easy way to invest to make a big break without checking your risk profile. If you are constantly chasing rates of returns on investments without taking a calculated risk, based on your own risk profile you might regret your decision later."

"Absolutely!" said Mrs. Trevor. "Although my husband Gabby and I were quite conservative at first, over time our risk tolerance grew. However we always took calculated risks when it came to investing and expanding our business."

"The reality is people often act out of fear or greed," I added. "The fear of losing money or the greed of making a ton of money. Every decision has consequences; therefore all aspects of an investment have to be considered before deciding how much risk to take. Your risk tolerance may vary depending on your age, your income, your total assets and your goals. Taking zero risk on your investments may be a good idea only if you are receiving a high rate of return, where the return after inflation and taxes is still acceptable to you. On the other hand if you are trying to double your money in a very short period of time with speculative, high risk investments it may not be the best option because you could easily lose most if not all of your principal. These types of investments are like gambling; unless you take a very small portion of your assets, maybe one to five percent and call it play money. This way you are aware of the risks and are not at a huge loss if you lose all of your capital.

"To accumulate wealth you must be aware of all the details we've just discussed. You must also take charge and make informed decisions."

A knock came on the door. Lunch was catered: colorful salads, sandwiches, refreshments and heavenly desserts. We took our time to enjoy the delicious meal, one another's company and our conversations. Nellie said she had never felt so enthralled about business. Right after lunch Georgina received a call from her lawyer about the separation agreement, so she excused herself. Mrs. Trevor and Sarah decided to leave as well. Terri, Nellie and I met with Nellie's husband to get a tour of the company. It was a delightful day.

We met three weeks later at my home with a nice surprise. Sarah brought her daughter Anusha to the meeting. Anusha was a beautiful, joyful and yet shy little girl. She sat next to her mother. Anusha took a liking to Mrs. Trevor and kept smiling at her. At some point Mrs. Trevor asked Anusha to sit beside her but she implied no. A few seconds later she ran to Mrs. Trevor, gave her a big hug, and sat on her lap.

The look of kindness and love on Sarah's face for Anusha was heartwarming to see. Sarah said that her neighbor always looked after Anusha when she came to our meetings but that day her neighbor had an important appointment.

Our topic for the day was taxation, which I thought may not be as fun for the group. I told Sarah it was a fabulous decision to bring her daughter.

Anusha ran back to Sarah and kissed her. "Mommy I love you."

The illuminated smiles on everyone's faces were magical.

"Sarah, your baby girl is special. She is adorable," said Mrs. Trevor.

Sarah looked down and humbly said: "Yah, thank you. It's so hard to know if I'm doing things right. I just want the best for my little angel."

Anusha hollered: "Thank you Mommy."

I welcomed everyone as we sat in our familiar seats. "Taxes are inevitable! Taxation is complicated. The tax system in Canada and the US is progressive, which means the more money you make, the more taxes you pay. Although tax rates are different in each province or state the system is similar. It is equally important to know your marginal tax rates. When you know a little about tax you become more aware of using the system to your benefit."

"You are not suggesting we know everything about taxes, are you?" Georgina asked.

"Not at all," I responded. "However, I believe being familiar with it is of great value to becoming financially independent. To simplify think of a tax return in four parts."

I walked to the whiteboard to list them, and Anusha followed me and stood next to me.

1. Your personal information
2. Your income from all sources for the year
3. All deductions and credits that you are eligible for
4. The tax calculation

"All other pages and forms are the supporting documents," I continued. "One area worth mentioning is investment income, which is categorized into three sections.

1. Interest income: This income is derived from interest made on investments such as savings and or checking accounts, bonds, guaranteed investments and any investments that generate interest. This interest is fully taxable.

2. Dividend income: This type of income is generated through profit paid from shares or stocks. Companies pay dividends to shareholders or mutual fund account holders. Stocks are either common or preferred. Divided income is taxed at a preferred rate which is taxed at a lower rate than interest income in Canada. Dividend income may be from Canadian or US companies or paid by foreign companies hence global dividends.

3. Capital Gains: These arise as a result of the disposition of capital property. The term property is used for an appreciating asset. Properties may be real estate, stocks (either preferred or common) and certain bonds which could trigger taxes upon sale or disposition of the asset. These assets are only taxable when they are sold; therefore, the increase in price is not taxed until they are cashed out.

"Get it?" Anusha asked everyone.

We all burst out laughing.

"To have wealth requires knowledge and constant learning," I added. You don't have to become an expert in the subject matter but at least have basic knowledge of taxation in order to make better decisions."

"I agree," Terri said. "It's always a good idea to have enough knowledge in order to ask the right questions when speaking to your financial planner or accountant."

Nellie looked surprised at this realization.

"In order to illustrate taxation on different investment types," I continued, "let's say for example, you receive $5,000 of interest income from your investments. The entire $5,000 will be added to your overall income and will be subject to tax based on your tax rate. However, dividend income is taxed differently in Canada. If you receive $5,000 of dividend income, the $5,000 will be grossed up and a credit will be given to offset part of the gross up. Depending on your overall income, dividends may be taxed at a lower rate than interest income. In Canada 50% of capital gains are taxable; which means if you have $5,000 of capital gains, only $2,500 will be taxable and you will have to add it to your income and pay tax accordingly. In the US however it depends on whether you have short term or long term capital gains."

"I am starting to enjoy the business conversations," Nellie expressed.

Mrs. Trevor leaned forward. "We bought a cottage for less than $100,000 many years ago and now it's worth almost $1 million. Once the cottage is sold or when I'm gone, the profit or capital gains will be taxable."

"A lot of taxes are payable then." Nellie looked at Mrs. Trevor with wonder.

Mrs. Trevor nodded.

"I have learned a little at a time," Georgina told us.

Terri shared her first investment experience.

"Capital gains are generated from the price increase on the asset. Years ago, I bought $25,000 worth of stocks at a price of $18.67 so I had 1339.046 shares ($25,000 ⊚ $18.67). The value of the shares increased to $21.24 per unit. I made a profit of $3,441.34!"

"How did you figure that out? And how do you remember all those details?" Nellie asked.

"Well the share price increased to $21.24 from $18.67, which is a profit of $2.57 per share. I had 1,339.046 units or shares (same thing) so if I multiply the profit per unit times the total units I get a profit of $3,441.34 which was taxable when I cashed out. And of course, I had to pay taxes. I remember this well because it was my first stock investment, and I made that profit in three months. Then I cashed out the whole investment, traded my old car and bought a new one."

"This is exciting, I wanna do that!" Sarah exclaimed.

"It is exciting," I said, "but what if the price of each share dropped to $14.67 from the purchase price of $18.67? If Terri was to sell her stocks she would have lost $4 per share, so multiply that by the 1,339 units she had and that would have been a loss of over $5,000. This is why your risk tolerance is important. If the price decreases, one option would be to hold on to your investment until the price comes back up again. For tax purposes capital losses are only used against capital gains, which means if you have a capital loss you cannot deduct it from your taxes. You have to wait until you have capital gains to offset against it."

Terri was smiling; it seemed she was still enjoying her investment profits from years ago.

I moved on to the next segment. "There are many tax shelters available, including educational plans."

"Sarah, can you manage to put any money aside for Anusha's future?" Mrs. Trevor asked.

"I want to, but I really can't afford it," Sarah replied sadly.

Anusha looked at Sarah and gave her a kiss on the cheek: "Don't be sad Mommy."

Georgina threw her hands in the air and said: "We finally got education plans for our two boys six months ago where the government gives you a grant."

"How is it going with your husband?" Mrs. Trevor asked.

"Please, I don't wanna talk about him," Georgina whined.

"So I can set one up for Anusha?" Sarah asked.

"Mommy I want to be a nurse."

Sarah hugged her daughter. "Honey, I thought you said you wanted to be a designer?"

"Yah, and a nurse. I wanna work in the hospital," Anusha smiled.

Mrs. Trevor chuckled. "You are such a brave girl. Can you nurse sick people?"

"Yeees. I want to give them medicine, so they get better," Anusha responded.

"I wish the world had more sweethearts like you who want to cure the world," Nellie said.

Anusha looked at Nellie and gave her a big smile.

"I am not sure if my husband has a plan set up for the kids. I am going to ask him," Nellie determined.

Mrs. Trevor looked very surprised.

"Nellie, you have children?"

"No, my husband's children," she replied.

Everyone looked at each other strangely.

"I think we have some sort of a trust plan. When his first wife died, a trust plan was set up for the twin girls," Nellie commented.

Mrs. Trevor asked: "How did she die?"

"During childbirth. The girls are seventeen now and at boarding school, preparing for university."

"How does that trust work?" Sarah asked.

"I am not really sure. I remember my husband mentioned something about not wanting to pay all the taxes," Nellie replied.

"I have set up some educational plans and trust accounts for my grandchildren and great grandchildren," Mrs. Trevor said.

"Mommy, why doesn't Grandma come and visit us?" Anusha asked.

Sarah hugged Anusha, an uncomfortable look crossing her face. "Honey, Grandma lives far away."

"Anusha, I live close by, maybe I can be your grandma," Georgina said to Anusha.

Anusha giggled. "Nooo."

"Why not?"

Anusha just smiled and shook her head.

"I'd like to know more about trust accounts. Can I open one for my nieces and nephews?" Terri asked.

"Yes," I said, "to have a trust you need three parties; the settlor or grantor, who sets up the trust (that would be you), the trustee who manages the trust and the beneficiary for whom the trust is opened, in this case your nieces or nephews or both. In most cases the settlor and the trustee are the same. The trust is considered an entity and has to pay its own taxes on the investment returns, although there may be some exceptions."

"Sounds good," Terri said.

I continued: "There are costs associated with a trust, which include the setup fee and an annual tax return. You must choose a trustworthy person who is of legal age and sound mind to be the trustee to be financially responsible for the funds.

"In addition to creating trusts there are also options to create holding companies depending on your objectives. In order to take advantage of tax deductions or tax shelters available you must consult an expert for your specific situation.

"Another tax shelter includes disability plans available for mentally or physically challenged individuals. You can also receive government support in addition to a disability trust."

Georgina seemed to have a question in mind.

"You may want to look into this for your son who is autistic, Georgina. Talk to your financial planner to find out more details as each situation is different."

Georgina thanked me and said she would.

"Plans are also available for first time home buyers, and each country, province or state may have different rules to qualify."

I was glad we had covered the entire fourth element in a financial plan. I offered ice cream as a treat after all that talk about taxes, and we chatted a little more. Anusha said she would like to come again, and I told her any time. We all said goodbye hoping to see each other again soon.

A few weeks passed. Everyone was busy. Terri asked if we would be interested in going to her friend's cottage for the day. She offered to pick us all up, but Georgina didn't want to go. She said the separation from her husband, taking care of her autistic child, and work was becoming difficult to manage. We decided to meet at my house for a couple of hours.

I arranged for us to gather in the dining room this time. I put out some appetizers, including a variety of nuts and dried fruits, on the table. I asked everyone how they were.

Nellie eagerly said: "I spoke to my husband about everything we've discussed so far. He said he will look into it and tell me everything I wanted to know."

"Very good," I acknowledged, "and remember it will take time to review all the information. Also ask him when he wants to retire."

Nellie perked up and threw her hands in the air. "Who knows?!"

"Today we're going to discuss Retirement Planning, the fifth element in a financial plan," I continued. "Think about at what age you want to retire: 65, 55 or perhaps 45 or 75? And why do you want to retire?"

Mrs. Trevor said: "My husband was still working in his eighties when he passed away."

"I can't think about retirement now when my world is upside down," Georgina expressed.

"Of course," Sarah reassured Georgina.

"Retirement means to withdraw from action. Unless you're ready to withdraw, why retire?" I said. "That's what I believe."

"I wanted to take a six-month sabbatical and travel the world. Maybe I should think about retiring early instead," Terri said.

I shared a story: "I know of a few people who were looking forward to retirement but unfortunately didn't make it that far. One woman worked really hard and accumulated a lot of wealth to secure her retirement, but the worst thing happened. She died a day before her retirement. The key is to enjoy life fully. You never know what life has in store for you. To plan for retirement is wise and wonderful provided you enjoy your youth before it's too late."

Mrs. Trevor nodded several times as everyone else pondered their future.

"The question is, what are your retirement dreams? What kind of life style do you have in mind? Where will you live? What will the source of your income be? Will your income be enough?"

"As much as I can't think about retirement, I am worried about it! Especially with my situation now." Georgina was concerned.

"If you plan well, things will work out," I assured her.

Sarah asked if I could elaborate on retirement planning.

I had positioned an easel in one corner of the dining room near where I sat. I listed some possible sources of retirement income:

- Government pensions
- Company pension plan (or widower's pension)
- Investment income including real estate
- Tax-sheltered investments such as RRSP, RRIF, TFSA, IRA, 401K, IPP
- Business income
- Inheritance

"The reason it's important to plan for retirement is to be able to live comfortably, as you will not have income from work. When we are younger we always think we have a lot of time before retirement and we may take life for granted."

"Or we are too busy worrying about our current situation and paying the bills, we disregard the future," Georgina shared.

Terri agreed. "We have a pension plan at work, but I can assure you, not everyone is participating and some live pay check to pay check."

"Yes, and we talked about budgeting, saving and investing. Once you write your goals and take those earlier steps in your financial plan, you can deliberately design your retirement and future," I added.

"My husband Gabby was concerned about the well-being of our employees and would invite professionals to speak to them from time to time."

"What a great idea!" Nellie reacted.

"As we have discussed how to create our desired life and live passionately we need to be cognizant of and take steps towards our future. Once we have our desired future in mind then we can start making a blueprint.

"Your retirement plan needs to include your desired future net worth and cash flow statements. We can start with key questions to consider regarding your pension plans:

- If you are currently working do you have a pension plan at work?
- Do you contribute to your pension plan or is it company contributions only?
- If you contribute to your pension plan how much of your annual income do you contribute? Maybe 4% or 6%?
- If you were to leave your company can you transfer your pension plan to your new employer's plan or your private plan such as an

RRSP, RRIF, IRA, 401K?

- If yes, how much money would you be able to transfer?
- What is the commuted value?
- Is it eligible to be transferred out? What are the terms and are they vested?
- Do you need to be with the company for a period of time before it is vested?
- Or do you have to leave it with the company and receive a monthly income at 65 or possibly at age 60?

The next crucial questions are:

- When you retire from your company how much pension will you receive from that company pension plan? What is the dollar value per month?
- Will that be enough to cover your expenses?
- What if you retire earlier than the normal retirement date, how much money will you receive at that time on a monthly basis?"

"Excellent questions." Terri sat up straight. She was scribbling notes. "I never thought of asking these types of questions until I changed companies. Even then my new company had a totally different pension plan and I had to make decisions I didn't know anything about. It was extremely stressful and, frankly, if I had been aware of my pension options before leaving that first company I would have had more funds accumulated in the plan."

"I don't know the answers to any of those questions except we have some sort of a pension plan," Georgina added. "Tell me more."

"There are two main types of pension plans," I continued:

1. Defined benefits
2. Defined contributions

Defined benefits is a pension plan where your benefits at retirement are defined based on a formula. The amount depends on your years of service, your age and your income generally for the last five years of your employment before retirement. On the other hand, defined contributions is a plan where the amount of contributions per pay is set. For example, 6% of your pay goes to the plan and your company matches it 100% or 50%.

"Occasionally there is a hybrid of these two plans.

"An Individual Pension Plan (IPP) is available for business owners. If you own your business, will you be selling it upon retirement? If you own a few businesses who will be managing them upon your retirement?"

"What if you don't have any sort of pension plan?" Sarah asked.

"Thinking ahead, Sarah?" Nellie asked.

Sarah just smiled and shrugged.

"You will need to check government plans and pay close attention to your investment strategies," I explained. "Tax sheltered retirement plans are another vehicle to secure your retirement."

"I couldn't agree more," said Mrs. Trevor. "We planned our retirement well in advance.

I had promised to keep it short that night, so we enjoyed the appetizers and decided to have a glass of wine to toast to our future! We ended the evening quite cheerfully.

* * *

It was challenging to get all of us together at the same time. Six weeks later, Terri called everyone to ask if we could meet after dinner at her condo. She didn't want to leave her new puppy all alone. We agreed. Georgina said it was perfect because she wanted to bring her autistic son Eric.

I was relieved to hear about the puppy and Eric because we were going to discuss the last segment of a financial plan, and Estate Planning is not necessarily a joyful subject. Pets and children always add an element of lightheartedness.

When I arrived, Terri and her puppy came to greet me. The puppy was so fluffy and cute. Georgina was already there with seven-year-old Eric. Eric was a sweet, quiet boy. I just wanted to hug him. I asked Georgina if she would mind and she said to ask Eric. I approached him, said hello, and asked a few questions, but he didn't respond. Then I asked if I could hug him. He looked at me, raised his shoulders and then dropped them, so I hugged him, and he hugged me back.

By then everyone else had arrived. Terri had a gorgeous, modern, chic penthouse suite with an unobstructed view of the lake. We all sat in the living room watching the sunset. She offered us tea or coffee and dessert.

"Today we are going to wrap up our discussion on the sixth step of a financial plan, Wills & Estate," I said.

Sarah admired the view, and Mrs. Trevor said: "Perfect."

"What is an estate?" I started. "When one passes away, the remaining assets are called the estate. Some people couldn't care less what happens to their estate when they pass on, while others are quite concerned about who will get what and how much.

"It's crucial to have a written will. A will is a legal document where you state your wishes as to how your assets must be divided between your beneficiaries. The designation of beneficiaries is essential to distribute your assets. Without a will, assets are disbursed according to the laws in your province or state. Your will has to be properly drafted or updated to ensure your assets will be distributed according to your wishes with minimum applicable taxes."

"I don't think I have anything in my name; do I still need a will?" Nellie asked.

"Absolutely!" I responded. "When a person dies it's considered that the deceased has redeemed all their assets at once on the day of death according to tax laws. You may have certain assets such as paintings or other personal assets. In your particular case, Nellie, most likely you are one of the main beneficiaries of your husband's estate. What happens if you are both in a car accident, he dies first and a week later you pass?"

Nellie jolted, almost spilling her coffee.

"If you have a written will the process will be much easier. In your will you must appoint an executor (although two is better) or an estate trustee and one or more beneficiaries. The executor is responsible for paying off any debts, filing your final income tax return, paying all taxes, and distributing the assets to the beneficiaries. If you are the executor and distribute the assets to the beneficiaries prior to paying all of the taxes, you may be responsible for the taxes owed."

"I see your point. If the assets are in my name and I don't have a will then I won't have control over who receives the inheritance," Nellie confirmed.

"Yes, and before the assets are distributed, the will has to be probated. This means the court has to validate the last written will of the deceased. There are costs involved and the amount varies in each province or state," I added.

"When Gabby died it took us months to settle the estate even though he had an updated will, and everything was clearly and specifically drafted. It's an exhausting process," Mrs. Trevor said.

Sarah was listening with intense curiosity.

"Taxation on death is another critical part of a financial plan," I continued. "Options are available to defer taxes, especially if the properties are jointly owned or transferred to your spouse. Taxation on death can be complicated depending on the country and state or province the deceased resided in and their citizenship, especially if a dual citizen."

"It gets more complicated if you have underage children," Georgina blurted.

"If you wish to set up a trust upon death that must be written in your will as well," I added.

"In your will you can appoint a guardian for your underaged children. A guardian is the person who will legally take care of them, provide food, shelter and day to day living expenses. You can detail your child's living space, the schools you want them to attend and much more.

"For example, Sarah, if you left insurance funds for Anusha, you could set up a trust through your will and appoint a trustee who is of legal age and sound mind to look after the funds. It's essential to thoroughly trust the person who will manage your child's funds for her financial well-being. You must ask the trustee if they are willing to take on that responsibility."

"It makes sense, and definitely adds to peace of mind, in case something happens," Sarah confessed.

"What's the difference between a guardian and a trustee?" Georgina asked.

"A trustee is a person who is financially responsible for the funds allocated to a particular beneficiary. The trustee controls and handles all funds and decisions regarding how the money should be spent.

There are some government regulations on the nature and type of investments a trustee is allowed to participate in unless the trust agreement gives full power to the trustee regardless of regulations."

"I'm interested in legal matters. They're fun. So the guardian is just responsible for taking care of the kids, but the trustee handles the money?" Sarah asked.

"You got it," I said. "You make provisions in your will under a testamentary trust agreement as to how and when the trustee is able to use the funds."

"Can I use a testamentary trust to leave funds for my under aged nieces and nephews?" Terri was eager to know. "I don't want them to have access to all the money at the age of eighteen."

"Yes," I responded. "And a trustee may or may not be the same as the guardian for your underaged child. For example, Sarah let's say that your sister is excellent with children and knows how to take care of them; however, she may not be the best person for financial management of the funds. You may choose your brother-in-law or an aunt as a capable trustee. You give clear direction to the trustee on how you want them to handle the funds."

"I need to update my will especially because of Eric's situation and my separation," Georgina said.

"I want you to know that a testamentary trust is set up after a person's death based on their will. However an inter vivos trust, also known as a living trust, is set up during a person's lifetime in order to minimize taxes and probate fees in the financial planning process."

Sarah and Nellie had taken a lot of notes. I asked if anyone had a specific question. They said no, but that the information would take a while to digest.

Mrs. Trevor cleared her throat. "Everyone in my family uses the cottage and I am not sure how to address it in my will. I will have to leave it to all my children equally, which may be an issue."

"I understand. A Family Trust may be one option," I said. "It is also important to distinguish between joint tenancy and tenancy in common. For example, if you are a joint tenant on a property with your spouse, if it remains a joint tenancy upon your passing, your spouse will become the sole owner of that property. Upon their passing, the property will go to whoever they chose as their estate beneficiaries. Whereas if this property was held as tenants in common, when you pass, your percentage interest in the property would go to the estate beneficiaries named in your will."

"Not all of the children and spouses get along with each other. My worry is if one or two want to sell their part of the inheritance then they wouldn't be able to enjoy the cottage," Mrs. Trevor added.

"It's not an easy decision," I commented.

"Another point is your will becomes void if you get married but it will not become void if you divorce. In that case, it will just be read as if your ex-spouse died before you. That is the law here where we live but you must review your will to make sure it is up to date."

Sarah finished writing and said: "Well I thought I didn't have to worry about it 'cause I don't have any money, but I'm gonna get some insurance and do all the things we talked about just in case."

"Also find out about the common-law relationships versus marriage, including same sex relationships for your province, state or residency," I advised.

Sarah looked curious.

"I lived and worked in the US for a few years," Terri said. "I must check into the tax laws and possibly get another will."

"Have you heard of Succession Planning?" Mrs. Trevor asked.

"What? Success planning?" Sarah wondered and took a piece of dessert.

"When my husband died a large sum of taxes had to be paid and all the investments had to be transferred to my name. I became the sole shareholder of the company and I tell you there was so much to take care of. Although we had all the right plans and documents it still took a long time to settle. My oldest son and I were the executors. We drafted a succession plan because that son has helped expand the company and will definitely receive a bigger chunk of our company," Mrs. Trevor shared.

Nellie was listening intently, and Georgina went to check on Eric.

"Find out if your assets can go to your spouse without triggering any tax, although even with tax deferral it isn't always best to leave everything to your spouse, especially in blended families and second or third marriages," I said.

Nellie's eyes widened in fear at the words blended families.

"Another issue is upon your passing you may want to provide for your spouse during their lifetime, but you want the capital to go to your children when your spouse passes instead of your spouse's beneficiaries. In this case a spousal trust may be established."

"Now I realize how important it is for me to pay attention and understand all of this," Nellie commented.

"Trusts are beneficial, for example if you have a wild child who may inherit your hard earned dollars. There is also a Henson trust if you have a disabled child. Trusts are effective in establishing when and how the funds will go to your beneficiaries," I added.

Georgina commented as she walked back into the living room: "I'm going to look into trusts for Eric. I think I may have a bigger problem than I was willing to admit."

"Eric is adorable," I complimented. "Of course it's always a good idea to explore all your options. If your children are below the age of majority you should recommend an alternate legal guardian and a trustee for their inheritance in your will. You can name two different people.

"If you have named your minor child as the beneficiary of your life insurance, pension, or registered plan, and you have not appointed a trustee, the funds may not be released by the financial institution until the child reaches the age of majority. In that case, the public guardian and trustee agree to act on the child's behalf, or somebody can apply for a court order to seek financial guardianship."

"I'm really starting to see the importance here. I think we take life for granted and never think it can happen to us," Georgina said humbly.

Nellie and Sarah agreed there was a lot to learn.

The sun had set by now. Terri told us how much she loved living in her condo and poured us more tea and coffee.

I asked if the group wanted to continue. They all concurred.

"A power of attorney known as POA is a legal document in which you authorize or give power to a person to act on your behalf while you are alive. Some powers of attorney are triggered by incapacity, while others can take effect immediately upon signing. There may be times when one gives power to another outside of incapacity reasons. The person you give power to act as your attorney must be of legal age and sound mind."

"I'm getting to like law but why do we need to know about this?" Sarah asked.

"Because this is part of your financial plan and you never know what life may bring!" I replied.

Mrs. Trevor sipped her tea. "It's absolutely necessary, especially for someone my age."

"Mrs. Trevor, you are sharp and articulate." Nellie smiled at her.

"You never know my dear. It's always good to be prepared," Mrs. Trevor replied.

A living will is an expression of your preferences for care in case of incapacity, while a power of attorney is actually appointing a substitute decision maker. The substitute decision maker appointed under a power of attorney is called the attorney, not the POA. The person granting the power of attorney is called the donor," I added.

"It's important to know these terms because when you appoint your attorneys, you let someone else make all sorts of decisions for you," Mrs. Trevor explained.

"That's right," I agreed, "and you want to make sure you are confident about your choices. POA's are used for Property, that is for your financial transactions or decisions and for Personal Care, which is your medical needs or decisions. It's extremely important that you choose someone you trust completely since typically you will be incapable when your attorney is required to exercise their authority. It is also recommended that you choose a secondary attorney to act jointly if necessary, or jointly and severely which means any of the named attorneys are eligible to act on your behalf independently."

Nellie, Georgina and Terri were glued to every word.

"It is, however, common to see living will terms incorporated into a power of attorney for personal care document, so the substitute decision maker is aware of those preferences. Although one document can include both your property and personal care attorneys, it's better to have two separate documents and to have them drafted by a legal professional even though that's not a legal requirement," I continued.

"My two eldest sons are my attorneys," Mrs. Trevor said.

"Very well. I'm going to have to change mine because I don't want my husband to make any decisions for me," Georgina burst out.

While Sarah was adding to her notes I continued: "If you have money in your investment or retirement account and you become incapacitated, no one can access your funds without a POA document unless they apply for financial guardianship by means of a court order. Your property attorney will have full control over your money so again it is crucial to choose the right person. The attorney cannot change your beneficiaries and cannot create or change your will."

I was relieved to have covered the most essential information in a financial plan and delighted to see how everyone had benefited.

"It's highly recommended," I said, "that you seek individual advice from a professional team. Financial planners will make sure you achieve your financial goals based on your financial circumstances, give advice and updated information. Lawyers draft your will and powers of attorney, set up legal documents for trusts if needed, and provide information on family law, divorce and other legal matters. Accountants will help with your taxes and business if you own one."

Everyone thanked me. They said had a lot to think about and many decisions to make. By this time Eric had come to Georgina and looked a bit tired. I asked if he had enjoyed playing with the puppy. He nodded with a smile.

We all hugged and said goodnight.

Your Financial Snapshot

FAMILY

Date:

Your Full Name:	
Your Date and Place of Birth:	
Your Home Address:	
Tel: Home/Cell:	
E-mail:	
Status: ❑ Single ❑ Married ❑ Divorced	
❑ Common-Law ❑ Separated ❑ Widowed	
Your Spouse's/Partner's Name & Date of Birth	
Ex -Spouse's Name:	

Children: Names and Dates of Birth

1)
2)
3)
4)
5)
6)

Grandchildren: Names and Dates of Birth

1)
2)
3)
4)
5)
6)

YOUR OCCUPATION

❑ Self-Employed   ❑ Retired   ❑ Not Working

❑ Disabled   ❑ Home-Maker

If retired, when did you retire?

If working when will you retire?

Name of Employer:

Address:

Tel:

Number of years:

If less than Three Years;
Previous Employer's Name & Address

Tel:

YOUR SPOUSE'S OCCUPATION

❑ Self-Employed   ❑ Retired   ❑ Not Working

❑ Disabled   ❑ Home-Maker

If retired, when did s/he retire?

If working when will s/he retire?

Name of Employer:

Address:

Tel:

Number of years:

If less than Three Years;
Previous Employer's Name & Address

Tel:

What are your financial Goals?

1)
2)
3)
4)
5)

1

127

CASH FLOW

INCOME	YOUR GROSS ANNUAL INCOME	YOUR SPOUSE'S GAI	YOUR GROSS MONTHLY INCOME	YOUR SPOUSE'S GMI	YOUR NET MONTHLY INCOME	YOUR SPOUSE'S NMI	TOTAL NET MONTHLY INCOME
Employment							
Self-Employment							
Company Pension							
Gov't Pension							
Rental Income							
Investment Income							
Other							
TOTAL INCOME:							

MONTHLY NET EXPENSES	YOURS	YOUR SPOUSE'S
Groceries		
Rent		
Mortgage		
Property Taxes		
Home insurance		
Electricity		
Gas		
Water		
Other		
Cable		
Internet		
Tel; landline + Cell		
Home Maintenance/Repairs		
Gardening/Snow removal		
Automobile Payments (loan)		
Automobile lease		
Automobile Insurance		
Automobile gas		

2

MONTHLY NET EXPENSES	YOURS	YOUR SPOUSE'S
Automobile parking		
Childcare		
Child Support		
Alimony		
Medical: Prescriptions, drugs		
Medical: Dental		
Medical: Eye Care		
Massage, acupuncture, etc.		
Education: School, courses		
Education: Supporting children		
Books, Subscriptions		
Clothing, shoes, bags		
Clothing- for children		
Grooming; (Hair cuts, make-up, etc.)		
Gifts (B-day's, Christmas, Anniversary, etc.)		
Insurance: Medical, health care		
Insurance: Life, Disability, Critical Illness, Long Term Care		
Entertainment: (dining out, concerts, movies, shows, etc.)		
Club membership (gym, associations, etc.)		
Holidays		
Hobbies (smoking, sports, etc.)		
Donations		
Loan Payments		
TOTAL EXPENSES:		

UNCOMMITTED INCOME
Total Net Income – Total Net Expenses =

3

NET WORTH STATEMENT

ASSETS	YOURS	YOUR SPOUSE'S	JOINT
CASH ASSETS			
Institution name – Chequing Acc't			
Institution name – Savings Acc't			
Institution name – Chequing Acc't			
Institution name – Savings Acc't			
Institution name – Deposit Acc't			
Institution name – Deposit Acc't			
TOTAL CASH ASSETS:			
INVESTMENT ASSETS			
Company name – # Stocks			
Company name – Forex trades			
Company name – Mutual Funds			
Company name – ETF's Other Funds			
Company name Corporate Bonds			
Government Bonds/Treasury Bills			
Cryptocurrency - type			
Institution name Guaranteed deposits			
Name – Mortgages Held			
Company Name - Life Insurance - Cash Value			
Company Name - Life Insurance - Cash Value			
Business Name/s – % Interest			
Business Name/s – % Interest			

4

ASSETS	YOURS	YOUR SPOUSE'S	JOINT
Real Property - Land			
Rental Property 1			
Rental Property 2			
Holding Company			
Trust Company			
Company name – RRSP/ RRIF Registered Retirement Savings Plan / Retirement Income Fund			
Company name – RRSP/ RRIF Registered Retirement Savings Plan / Retirement Income Fund			
Company name – RRSP/ RRIF Registered Retirement Savings Plan / Retirement Income Fund			
Company name – TFSA Tax Free Savings Account			
Company name – TFSA Tax Free Savings Account			
Company name – RESP Registered Education Savings Plan			
Company name – RESP Registered Education Savings Plan			
Company name – Educational Plan (Only if you own it and not your child)			
Company name – 401K			
Company name – 401K			
Company name – IRA Individual Retirement Account			
Pension plan – Commuted Value			
Company name – IPP Individual Pension Plan			
TOTAL INVESTMENT ASSETS:			

5

131

ASSETS	YOURS	YOUR SPOUSE'S	JOINT
PERSONAL ASSETS			
Principal Residence			
Cottage			
Automobile			
Automobile			
Truck			
Boat			
Trailer, Motor Cycle, etc.			
Snow mobile			
Furnishings			
Art Collection			
Other Collection (stamp, coin, gun, train)			
Jewellery			
Accounts Receivable			
TOTAL PERSONAL ASSETS:			
TOTAL ASSETS:			

LIABILITIES	YOURS	YOUR SPOUSE'S	JOINT
LONG TERM LIABILITIES			
Lender's name - Mortgage (1) Renewal Date, interest rate, amortization			
Lender's name - Mortgage (2) Renewal Date, interest rate, amortization			

6

LIABILITIES	YOURS	YOUR SPOUSE'S	JOINT
Lender's name - Mortgage on Rental Property (1) Renewal Date, interest rate, amortization			
Lender's name - Mortgage on Rental Property (2) Renewal Date, interest rate, amortization			
Lender's name - Loan 10+ years Purpose? Renewal Date, interest rate, amortization			
Lender's name - loan 10+ years Purpose? Renewal Date, interest rate, amortization			
TOTAL LONG TERM LIABILITIES			
SHORT TERM LIABILITIES			
Lender's name - Line of Credit Interest rate, secured ☐ Y ☐ N Against what collateral			
Lender's name - Line of Credit Interest rate, secured ☐ Y ☐ N Against what collateral			
Lender's name - Loan purpose, Renewal Date, interest rate, term			
Lender's name - Loan purpose, Renewal Date, interest rate, term			
Lender's name - Loan purpose, Renewal Date, interest rate, term			
Institution – credit card type, interest rate, limit			
Institution – credit card type, interest rate, limit			
Institution – credit card type, interest rate, limit			
Institution – credit card type interest rate, limit			
Accounts Payable – to whom Interest rate, term			
Taxes Payable - overdue Interest rate, term			
TOTAL SHORT TERM LIABILITIES			
TOTAL LIABILITIES			

7

133

TOTAL ASSETS
Total Assets = Total Cash Assets + Total Investment Assets + Total Personal Assets =

TOTAL LIABILITIES
Total Liabilities = Total Long Term Liabilities + Total Short Term Liabilities =

NET WORTH
Net Worth = Total Assets − Total Liabilities =

NOTES

9

INSURANCE POLICIES

LIFE INSURANCE

Insured's Name

Insurance Company Name

Coverage amount

Type: Permanent ❑ Y ❑ N   Term ❑ Y ❑ N

Term; Renewal & Expiry date

Other Benefits

Cash Value

Total Death Benefit

Beneficiaries and percentage share

1)

2)

3)

Payment Amount Monthly _____ Annual _____

Individually owned ❑ Y ❑ N Group ❑ Y ❑ N

Date of Issue & Policy Number

LIFE INSURANCE

Insured's Name

Insurance Company Name

Coverage amount

Type: Permanent ❑ Y ❑ N   Term ❑ Y ❑ N

Term; Renewal & Expiry date

Other Benefits

Cash Value

Total Death Benefit

Beneficiaries and percentage share

1)

2)

3)

Payment Amount Monthly _____ Annual _____

Individually owned ❑ Y ❑ N Group ❑ Y ❑ N

Date of Issue & Policy Number

LIFE INSURANCE

Insured's Name

Insurance Company Name

Coverage amount

Type: Permanent ❑ Y ❑ N   Term ❑ Y ❑ N

Term; Renewal & Expiry date

Other Benefits

Cash Value

Total Death Benefit

Beneficiaries and percentage share

1)

2)

3)

Payment Amount Monthly _____ Annual _____

Individually owned ❑ Y ❑ N Group ❑ Y ❑ N

Date of Issue & Policy Number

LIFE INSURANCE

Insured's Name

Insurance Company Name

Coverage amount

Type: Permanent ❑ Y ❑ N   Term ❑ Y ❑ N

Term; Renewal & Expiry date

Other Benefits

Cash Value

Total Death Benefit

Beneficiaries and percentage share

1)

2)

3)

Payment Amount Monthly _____ Annual _____

Individually owned ❑ Y ❑ N Group ❑ Y ❑ N

Date of Issue & Policy Number

10

DISABILITY INSURANCE

Insured's Name

Insurance Company Name

Coverage Term

Monthly Benefit

Waiting Period

Benefit Period

Other Benefits

Payment Amount Monthly _____ Annual _____

Individually owned ❑ Y ❑ N Group ❑ Y ❑ N

Date of Issue & Policy Number

DISABILITY INSURANCE

Insured's Name

Insurance Company Name

Coverage Term

Monthly Benefit

Waiting Period

Benefit Period

Other Benefits

Payment Amount Monthly _____ Annual _____

Individually owned ❑ Y ❑ N Group ❑ Y ❑ N

Date of Issue & Policy Number

CRITICAL ILLNESS

Insured's Name

Insurance Company Name

Coverage amount

Coverage Term

Payment Amount Monthly _____ Annual _____

Other Benefits

Individually owned ❑ Y ❑ N Group ❑ Y ❑ N

Date of Issue & Policy Number

CRITICAL ILLNESS

Insured's Name

Insurance Company Name

Coverage amount

Coverage Term

Payment Amount Monthly _____ Annual _____

Other Benefits

Individually owned ❑ Y ❑ N Group ❑ Y ❑ N

Date of Issue & Policy Number

LONG TERM CARE

Insured's Name

Insurance Company Name

Coverage amount

Benefit Period

Indexed ❑ Y ❑ N

Date of Issue & Policy Number

Payment Amount Monthly _____ Annual _____

LONG TERM CARE

Insured's Name

Insurance Company Name

Coverage amount

Benefit Period

Indexed ❑ Y ❑ N

Date of Issue & Policy Number

Payment Amount Monthly _____ Annual _____

HEALTH CARE

Insured's Name

Insurance Company Name

Coverage amount

Medical Coverage

Dental Coverage

Payment Amount Monthly _____ Annual _____

Individually owned ❑ Y ❑ N Group ❑ Y ❑ N

HEALTH CARE

Insured's Name

Insurance Company Name

Coverage amount

Medical Coverage

Dental Coverage

Payment Amount Monthly _____ Annual _____

Individually owned ❑ Y ❑ N Group ❑ Y ❑ N

11

LIABILITY INSURANCE

Insured's Name

Insurance Company Name

Coverage type – purpose

Coverage amount

Term and expiry date

Date of Issue & Policy Number

Payment Amount Monthly _____ Annual _____

AUTOMOBILE INSURANCE

Insured's Name

Make, Model and Year

Insurance Company Name

Insurance Policy Number

Issue Date and Expiry Date

Liability Coverage

Deductible

Riders

Payment Amount Monthly _____ Annual _____

PROPERTY INSURANCE

Insured's Name

Insurance Company Name

Insurance Policy Number

Issue Date and Expiry Date

Coverage amount

Liability Coverage

Deductible

Riders

Payment Amount Monthly _____ Annual _____

LIABILITY INSURANCE

Insured's Name

Insurance Company Name

Coverage type – purpose

Coverage amount

Term and expiry date

Date of Issue & Policy Number

Payment Amount Monthly _____ Annual _____

AUTOMOBILE INSURANCE

Insured's Name

Make, Model and Year

Insurance Company Name

Insurance Policy Number

Issue Date and Expiry Date

Liability Coverage

Deductible

Riders

Payment Amount Monthly _____ Annual _____

PROPERTY INSURANCE

Insured's Name

Insurance Company Name

Insurance Policy Number

Issue Date and Expiry Date

Coverage amount

Liability Coverage

Deductible

Riders

Payment Amount Monthly _____ Annual _____

NOTES

12

ADDITIONAL INSURANCE POLICIES

AUTOMOBILE INSURANCE

PROPERTY INSURANCE

BOAT INSURANCE

SNOWMOBILE INSURANCE

MOTORCYCLE INSURANCE

LEGACY AND RECORDS

WILL
Do you have a **Will**?   ❑ Y ❑ N
How many wills do you have?
Which country and state/province were they drafted?
Date Your will/s was last updated?
Who is it kept with and the location?
Who are the Executors and relationships to you:
1)
2)
3)
Who are the beneficiaries of your estate? Be Specific and the percentage share:
1)
2)
3)
4)
5)
6)
7)
Have you clearly indicated the following in your will and their responsibilities?
Guardian   ❑ Y ❑ N ❑ N/A
Trustee   ❑ Y ❑ N ❑ N/A
Have you set up a Trust   ❑ Y ❑ N
For who?

POWER OF ATTORNEY
Do you have a **Power of Attorney for Medical?** ❑ Y ❑ N   How many POA's _____
Their names and your relationship with them:
When was it last updated?
Where is the POA document located?
Do you have a **Power of Attorney for Property?** ❑ Y ❑ N   How many POA's _____

Their names and your relationship with them:
When was it last updated?
Where is the POA document located?
Do you have a Lawyer/Notary Public? ❑ Y ❑ N
Name & Tel:
Address & E-Mail:
Do you have a Financial Planner ?   ❑ Y ❑ N
Name & Tel:
Address & E-Mail:
Do you have an Accountant?   ❑ Y ❑ N
Name & Tel:
Address & E-Mail:
Do you have a Tax Preparer?   ❑ Y ❑ N
Name & Tel:
Address & E-Mail:

YOUR RECORDS
Where do you keep them?
Birth Certificate #:
Social Insurance/ Social Security #:
Country of Citizenship and #:
Your Passport #:
Marriage/Divorce Certificate #:
Marriage Contract: ❑ Y ❑ N
Separation Contract: ❑ Y ❑ N
Pre-nuptial Agreement: ❑ Y ❑ N
Military Discharge & Country:
Association/ Membership:
Passwords:
Contracts: With who and where
Do you have a safety Deposit Box?   ❑ Y ❑ N
Location:
Where is the Key:

14

140

FUNERAL ARRANGEMENTS	People to be contacted in case of Death:
Have you made Funeral Arrangements ❏ Y ❏ N	Name & Tel:
	Name & Tel:
Do you have a cemetery plot? ❏ Y ❏ N	Name & Tel:
Location & Tel:	Name & Tel:
Do you like to be cremated? ❏ Y ❏ N	**Notes:**
Do you want to donate your Organs? ❏ Y ❏ N	
Have you indicated this in your will? ❏ Y ❏ N	
Have you informed anyone? ❏ Y ❏ N	
Your Doctor? Name	
Next of Kin? Name	
Your Executor? Name	
Have you decided on Health Care Directive/To End Life? ❏ Y ❏ N	
Have you indicated this in your will? ❏ Y ❏ N	
Have you informed anyone? ❏ Y ❏ N	
Your Doctor? Name	
Next of Kin? Name	
Your Executor? Name	

Your Risk Profile

Your Name:	Date:

1) WHAT IS THE PURPOSE OF YOUR INVESTMENT?

❑ a) Passive Income

❑ b) Current Income

❑ c) Increase Your wealth

❑ d) Retirement

2) WHAT IS THE TIME HORIZON FOR YOUR YOURINVESTMENT?

❑ a) 1-2 Years

❑ b) 3-5 Years

❑ c) 6-10 Years

❑ d) 10 Years or More

3) HOW MUCH RISK CAN YOU TAKE FOR YOUR INVESTMENT?

❑ a) I cannot lose any of my principal capital

❑ b) I can lose a small amount of my principal capital temporary provided I get a higher return

❑ c) I can tolerate fluctuations in my principal capital provided I get a higher return

❑ d) I can take fluctuations in my principal capital provided I get a higher return

1

4) **What is Your Investment style?**

    ❏ a) I am a very Conservative Investor

    ❏ b) I am a Moderately Conservative Investor

    ❏ c) I am a Moderately Aggressive Investor

    ❏ d) I am an Aggressive Investor

5) **What is Your Risk Style?**

    ❏ a) I cannot take any risks in my investments

    ❏ b) I can take Moderate risks in my investments

    ❏ c) I can take some risks in my investments

    ❏ d) I can take a lot of risks in my investments

6) **What rate of return do you expect to make annually on your 100,000 investment?**

    ❏ a) I expect to make 1-3% growing my investment to $101,000-$103,000

    ❏ b) I expect to make 4-6% growing my investment to $104,000-$106,000

    ❏ c) I expect to make 7-10% growing my investment to $107,000-$110,000

    ❏ d) I expect to make 11-15% growing my investment to $111,000-$115,000

7) **How much can your $100,000 investment return fall in one year?**

    ❏ a) I am comfortable with a fall of 1-3 % in one year; leaving it to $99,000-$97,000

    ❏ b) I am comfortable with a fall of 4-6 % in one year; leaving it to $96,000-$94,000

    ❏ c) I am comfortable with a fall of 7-10 % in one year; leaving it to $93,000-$90,000

    ❏ d) I am comfortable with a fall of 11-15 % in one year; leaving it to $89,000-$85,000

8) **What is your expectation when you invest?**

    ❏ a) When I invest I expect no losses whatsoever

    ❏ b) When I invest I expect to gain a return right away

    ❏ c) When I invest I am worried about losing my principal capital

    ❏ d) When I invest I am thinking I am taking a risk to make money

9) **What calculated risk can you take for your $100,000 investment?**

    ❏ a) 100-0% chance with a 2% return – your money becomes $102,000 guaranteed in one year

    ❏ b) 80-20% chance with an 8% return – your money becomes $108,000 or $92,000 in one year

    ❏ c) 65-35% chance with a 15% return – your money becomes $115,000 or $85,000 in one year

    ❏ d) 50-50% chance with a 30% return – your money becomes $150,000 or $50,000 in one year

2

10) The rates of returns for most Investments fluctuate every year. In a 15- year time horizon which investment type are you comfortable with?

❑ a) Average 15-year return 3% provided maximum return on any one year; gain +4% and loss -1%

❑ b) Average 15- year return 6% provided maximum return on any one year; gain +20% and loss -15%

❑ c) Average 15-year return 10% provided maximum return on any one year; gain +40% and loss -35%

❑ d) Average 15-year return 15% provided maximum return on any one year; gain +50% and loss 50%

3

YOUR INVESTMENT PURPOSE				
QUESTION 1	A	B	C	D
YOUR INVESTMENT PURPOSE				

YOUR TIME HORIZON					
QUESTION 2	A	B	C	D	SCORE
YOUR TIME HORIZON	1	2	3	4	A =

YOUR RISK TOLERANCE					
QUESTION 3-10	A	B	C	D	SCORE
YOUR RISK STYLE	1	2	3	4	
Question 3					
Question 4					
Question 5					
Question 6					
Question 7					
Question 8					
Question 9					
Question 10					
TOTAL				(add 3 to 10)	B=

To find your Risk Profile; place your score A vertically down and place your score B horizontally.

YOUR RISK PROFILE						
B / A	YOUR TIME HORIZON	8-11	12-16	17-24	25- 29	30- 36
1	1-2 Years	❑ Very Conservative	❑ Very Conservative	❑ Conservative	❑ Conservative	❑ Moderate
2	2-5 Years	❑ Very Conservative	❑ Very Conservative	❑ Conservative	❑ Conservative	❑ Aggressive
3	5-10 Years	❑ Very Conservative	❑ Conservative	❑ Moderate	❑ Aggressive	❑ Very Aggressive
4	10 Years +	❑ Very Conservative	❑ Conservative	❑ Moderate	❑ Aggressive	❑ Very Aggressive

YOUR RISK PROFILE IS:	

4

Chapter 5

Your Wellness

5

The anticipation was building. As per my suggestion we had decided to visit a unique, full-service spa to celebrate Sarah's twenty-first birthday. We all shared the cost of her spa package as a present. Everyone was excitedly texting back and forth the day before.

When we met at the spa at ten that morning, Mrs. Trevor had an animated smile on her face.

"Oh my goodness; I haven't been to a spa for at least ten years."

"I love spas. I go often," Nellie said joyously.

Terri admitted that although spas were rejuvenating, she always ended up in the gym.

Sarah looked at us one by one. "I am so thankful for this present," she said. She covered her mouth with her hands and swallowed, held her tears and continued: "You guys doing this for me means a lot. No one has ever done anything like this for me before."

Georgina gave her a big hug. "What are friends for, huh? We're practically family now." Everyone gathered closer and held one another. Then Georgina said: "I know it's pricey coming here, but I didn't wanna miss it. My husband does what he wants, and I do what I want."

"Good for you!" Terri burst out.

We had all booked different services throughout the day. Some of us started with a full body massage. Stress, worry and negative feelings produce toxins in the body. Massage is certainly one way to release them and prevent buildup.

After an hour and a half we met in a private lounge area for green tea. The women's faces were relaxed and peaceful.

Georgina told a joke and we all laughed. Sarah couldn't stop. That in turn made Georgina laugh more, until she couldn't stop either. We kept laughing and laughing. As soon as it ended, Georgina would burst into laughter again. Laughter is indeed contagious!

"I think this massage was exactly what my body needed. All the tension... My husband hasn't touched me in months," she chuckled sadly. "Maybe this laughter was good for my pent up emotions."

Nellie patted her arm.

I noticed tears in Terri's eyes. She was usually calm, composed and alert, but today she looked quite vulnerable.

"Terri?" I asked.

"You know," she said, "my father died of heart attack last year and I've never mourned his loss. I loved him so much. My parents divorced when I was four years old."

Everyone was quiet.

"I am always busy at work and need to be focused. Today's the first time in ages I've truly relaxed."

Mrs. Trevor took the lead. "My dear you need time, to let go and accept the loss. Cherish the memories you had with your father."

Terri brushed tears from her eyes and said she thought she would go to the meditation room for the next session.

"Are you relaxed enough to meditate?" I asked.

She shook her head.

"If you'd like to reflect and sit with your emotions, that's great," I said, "but you need to be relaxed to meditate. It's better to use techniques to relax the muscles and the body when we are not in a peaceful state. If you are emotionally charged the best thing to do is to relax, not meditate. How about some energy work with a practitioner first?"

She agreed and left the lounge.

Mrs. Trevor went for a head and shoulder massage. Sarah went for a body wrap treatment and I decided to meditate. It was the perfect time because my body was already so relaxed.

I went into one of the meditation rooms. No one was there. Soft instrumental music was playing, and the scent of essential oils was heavenly. I gave gratitude for being there and took a few deep breaths. I focused on my breath in order to start relaxing my body deeply. I began with a balancing breath of five in breaths, held for five, and five out breaths. I focused on my head first and relaxed it, then focused my breath on my face, my arms, then one by one my chest, my abdomen and down my legs to my toes. A few thoughts kept filtering through my mind, but I kept focusing on my breath to increase the gap between each thought. I decided to add a visual to my breath. With each inhale I imagined pure white oxygen entering my body, welcoming the beauty of life in me. This type of inhale cleansed and rejuvenated my body even more deeply. Then with each exhale I imagined releasing all negativity, and carbon dioxide leaving my body. I repeated this for a few minutes, until I was completely and utterly relaxed yet quite alert.

Meditation is a practice where you may direct your mind to a specific thought or object to increase awareness, possibly connect to Source and receive clear visions, answers or information. You may also use meditation to get clarity on your emotions or mental state.

Meditation can begin once the body is in a deep state of relaxation. A variety of meditation techniques are available. One of these is total silence: no sound, no access to smartphones, radio, TV or any sort of computer. Once we are very comfortable, the activation can start. It's only during these meditative times that creativity is more accessible because we are more in touch with our inner feelings and emotions, and we are able to solve problems much more readily.

It has been proven that when we meditate on a regular basis our body starts relaxing in a profound way, and new pathways to our brain open up.

That day I was drawn to Contemplation, a great technique to ask my body and higher self for information.

Chakras or energy fields are an ancient concept of the life force that surrounds us. There are seven main chakras or vortex of energy centers around our bodies. As I scanned my body with visualization and breathing, I envisioned each, in order. The Root chakra, emanating from the base of my spine, is associated with the color red, representing security. It is the emotional energy Allowance that allows flow, the movement of all things, what I allow and what I do not. The Sacral chakra, below my navel, associated with the color orange, represents creativity and pleasure, with an emotional energy of Allegiance providing direction. Then the Solar Plexus, yellow, is Will and Power, the force that gathers things together, the attractive force that is, and the emotion of what I control and what controls me. The Heart chakra emanating from my heart, with the color green, is Love, which represents how densely things are brought together. The Throat chakra, blue and associated with expression, is the emotional energy of Harmony; it knows the proper proportion seeking to be my conscience and balance. The sixth chakra the Third Eye, in the middle of my forehead, indigo blue, and is Knowledge which is all that has been; emotions and experiences with the five senses. The seventh chakra, the Crown at the top of my head, associated with gold or purple, connection to the Divine, is Wisdom, the energy of all that may be.

I began a Contemplation exercise, asking a question of Allowance, the first chakra, then based on the answer, I asked the second chakra for an answer, and continued all the way to the Wisdom, the seventh chakra.

I asked about this book *Joyous Wealth*:

Allowance: What do I allow?

Allegiance: What am I in allegiance with?

Will & Power: What do I control and co-operate with?

Love: What is the glue that holds?

Harmony: What should I be conscious of and how much?

Knowledge: What knowledge can I use?

Wisdom: What does the future look like?

The answer I received after going through the process three times filled me with joy and purpose:

"Just let it flow, ten to twelve chapters, show millions passion and compassion, get on the media, take ownership, speak of ancient wisdom, use the Divine teachings, power to change, how to receive, talk about the details and characters in the book, let your wisdom shine through. Establish that you are the go to person."

I was in awe of the answers I received. It took less than twenty minutes but felt like I was in the meditation room for more than an hour. I slowly got up and headed towards the lounge.

I sat quietly in the lounge for some time, soaking in the aroma. The rest of our group filtered in to our private oasis at lunch time, where the chef had prepared a special meal for us.

Mrs. Trevor raised her glass. "Here is a toast to our birthday girl. Wishing you a life filled with happiness, prosperity and a journey to empowerment."

Filled with the power of those words, everyone smiled and raised their glasses.

Sarah laughed out loud with joy. "Thank you, I really appreciate it."

Mrs. Trevor continued. "We are blessed to share this meal together and be in one another's company."

We indulged in the fresh and nutritious food. A feeling of tranquility came over us; there was nothing to say or do except be in the moment and enjoy the delicious meal.

After lunch Terri went to the steam room. Mrs. Trevor wanted to sit in the lounge and read a book. Nellie decided to go to yoga but had to wait a while as she had just finished lunch. She wandered around the art gallery. Georgina chose to have tea, so she stayed in the lounge with Mrs. Trevor.

I noticed Sarah looking at me.

"Do you want to go to the sauna?" I asked.

"I'd love to."

Once we settled in, inhaling the eucalyptus scent, Sarah confessed she was estranged from her mother.

"Has Anusha met her grandmother?"

"Yes, twice. My sister and I went to the mall, and behind my back my sister had asked our mom to meet us there," Sarah complained. "I got really upset with my sister. She said she just wanted us to be a family again and wanted my mom to meet Anusha."

"How did it go? And how do you feel about that?"

"My mom was so happy to see Anusha she just hugged her, and Anusha instantly gravitated towards her. She put her head on my mom's shoulder and stayed there for a minute."

"That is good, isn't it?" I asked.

"I don't know. I'm afraid my mom is gonna take Anusha away from me."

"Why do you think that, Sarah?"

"Because I use drugs," Sarah confessed again. "Then I saw her a second time, on the street where I live."

"Did she see Anusha?" I asked.

"Oh yeah. Anusha yelled 'Grandma' and ran to her," Sarah replied.

I paused for a moment: "Well, how about you start communicating with your mother and restart a new relationship?"

"I don't know if I can. They really hurt me." Sarah took a breath. "My parents had different personalities; they fought all the time. My father couldn't hack it anymore. He hooked up with a twenty-five year old. My brothers are older than her, you know, and that broke my mother's heart. I was seventeen and pregnant. My mom kept yelling at me, saying nasty stuff, so I took off." She paused and said: "I need a fix."

"Sarah, just take deep breaths. Hang in there for now."

After a minute or two she continued: "I believed in family unity, even though it wasn't perfect. But I am heartbroken," she whispered.

I told her that I understood, and we sat quietly in the sauna for a few minutes.

"Emotional Resilience is an important key in handling stress," I began. "There is a relationship between thoughts, feelings and actions. You can change your life experience by shifting your beliefs. The ability to reframe your mind chatter in the heat of the moment adds to resilient thinking skills. We can ask ourselves the A, B, Cs of Cognitive Reprogramming."

I listed them:

A What are the facts? A is the Activating Event
B What are your thoughts and beliefs? B is Belief
C How did it make you feel or what did it make you do? C is the Consequence

"Sarah, let's start with A. The fact is that your father left, your mother was devastated after being married for what, like thirty years, and she took it out on you. B, you thought and believed you were not supported whatsoever when you were pregnant and needed comfort. C, it made you feel betrayed and angry. Correct?"

She choked up. "Yeah," she said.

I continued: "Let's take the same scenario, the Activating Event is the same because the facts don't change. But now shift your Belief: My mom wanted the best for me, and she was devastated herself. She was trying to protect me. My father knew all about responsibility and had had enough, so he took off and he tried to protect me by not accepting my choice.

"You felt betrayed and angry which is C, the Consequence. By shifting your thoughts can you perhaps feel compassion or love? Can you see how shifting the B, your Belief system, can possibly shift your experience?"

Sarah was deep in thought, dripping with perspiration from the sauna and processing emotions.

After a minute or two she said: "My mind keeps going. It's so hard to stop all these thoughts right now, but I get what you mean."

I continued: " Of course, and when you pay attention to your mind chatter, the more you become aware of your thoughts, the more resilient you can become. Over time your resilient thinking skills will provide you with Emotional Resilience.

"To be compassionate without prejudice or judgment is one of the highest attributes of human achievement, known as forgiveness. It can be one of the most difficult feelings to deal with. Do you know that when you don't forgive someone, regardless of the heart ache and despair that person may have caused you, it's your feelings that are affected?"

"How so?" Sarah asked.

"Because you are the one holding on to the feelings of resentment and anger. Those are negative emotions, and they hold space inside your body. This negativity takes away from the flow of your energy," I responded. "Put yourself in their shoes and see if you can feel how they thought they had only one choice and acted from that place, because they felt fear or were at a weak moment in their lives. Now feel their pain or fear or maybe arrogance, which by the way comes from fear. Practice the scene until you gain an understanding of the other person's thinking. When you understand the behavior, ask yourself if you can forgive. Once you forgive you will notice a tremendous amount of energy within you is released, and this can make you feel free. Keep trying this until you actually feel the forgiveness. It is an incredible sensation."

She agreed, and we decided to leave the sauna as we had already been there for more than thirty minutes. We took a quick shower and when we got back to the lounge, Mrs. Trevor was napping on her chair and Georgina wasn't there.

Sarah said: "Thank you so much, that was very helpful. I am going to try this meditation class. I don't really know how it works. What do you think?"

"Sarah there are a variety of meditation techniques and with practice you can build up your evolutionary brain. But before you do that it's best to use relaxation techniques. These include getting a massage, spending quality time with family or friends, being intimate with your partner and many more."

"Really? Oh wow. OK then, I should go for a massage?"

"If you wish. It's your day!"

She smiled and asked if I had any last minute advice.

"You can also increase peace of mind through physical exercise, as it releases chemicals, telling the body it is in a relaxed state and there is no threat. Physical exercise can be things like working out in the gym, going for walks, dancing which is your favorite, gymnastics, yoga, chi gong or a variety of exercises that require actual physical work. Using any sort of relaxation will reduce the limbic reactions to stress."

"I like that," she said.

"And remember when you're more involved in life and participate fully it increases your joy in life. Participation in life releases the joy hormones and oxytocin," I added.

She left looking happy and radiant. "See you in a bit," she said.

As I was nodding I saw Nellie walk back into the lounge.

"They have beautiful art work and sculptures here. I think some are for sale," she said. Before I was able to respond, she continued. "I'll go to yoga tomorrow. Can I ask you something?"

We ordered more green tea and sat next to each other on the beautiful purple chaise lounge.

Nellie kept licking and lightly biting her lips, which told me she was going to share something sensitive and uncomfortable. She clasped her hands.

"It's quite private." She paused. "I am not sure why I am thinking about this today, after so many years."

"Nellie, what we discuss stays between us. Obviously something is bothering you."

She looked up at the ceiling and said: "I am not sure where to start, so I will tell you the short version."

"Whatever you'd like to share, I am here for you."

"I appreciate that." She took a deep breath. "When I was very young I was molested and sexually abused." Her body froze, goosebumps popped all over her arms, and her eyes became lifeless for a few moments.

In order to bring her back to the present I said: "Nellie, have a sip of tea."

Her body shook. "Oh thank you." She sipped. "I dealt with it more than ten years ago. I went to therapy and actually forgave the person who violated me."

"I am impressed, Nellie. That's not an easy thing to do."

"Yes," she said. "I don't want to talk about the details. I'm just startled that I would remember it today after many years." She took another sip of tea. Although she was exuding love, the expression on her face was vulnerable and frightened.

"Sometimes when the body is truly relaxed, unresolved emotions surface," I said.

"But I went through the process with my therapist."

"Past experiences are still within us and may come to surface from time to time so we can look at them from a different perspective. Emotions are never deleted from our subconscious." Nellie was listening intently. " Have you heard of Emotional Reserves?" I asked.

She said no.

"Emotional Reserves are like the financial reserves we talked about. When unexpected things happen, such as loss of a job or income, if you can't work due to illness or injury and your regular income is stopped or delayed, or when an unexpected big bill comes in, you resort to your financial reserves.

"Emotional Reserves are emotions you can access when feeling down, sad, or disappointed, or when you are experiencing some sort of loss. Although you experience new things all the time and no one experience is necessarily the same as the other, I believe you can use your Emotional Reserves to get over the challenge."

Her shoulders relaxed as if she saw hope.

"Let's say you know how it feels to be loved, or you know the feeling of being able to afford to buy what you want, or that you have a wonderful relationship with your spouse or a family member, or you know how it feels to be happy, to be supported by your surroundings, you know how it feels to laugh and be empowered and you know how to be joyful. Then all of a sudden something unexpected happens which takes away your joy, your happiness and your vivacity. After feeling these unpleasant feelings and accepting the situation, the best thing is to refer to your internal resources of empowerment, rise above the challenge, feel forgiveness, happiness and excitement, and tap into your Emotional Reserves in order to get your vibrant energy back and deal with it in a calm and peaceful manner.

"Now, Nellie, you can imagine whatever is relevant to you in your situation. In order to get a broader perspective, think of or imagine what Emotional Reserves you can access."

She thought about it briefly and said: "Yes, I am going to do that. Thank you." She left the lounge to freshen up.

I was overwhelmed with the stories I had heard that day. First Terri, then Sarah and now Nellie. I wasn't expecting any of this and yet it was good. Everyone felt psychologically safe enough for emotions to come up so that they would have a chance to deal with them.

Mrs. Trevor was awake by then and smiled gently at my overwhelmed expression. She looked at me for a good fifteen seconds without a word. It felt like she was saying: 'This is life with its good, its beauty and its pain.' I looked at her with teary eyes and dropped my head while rubbing my forehead and reflecting.

Our thoughts have tremendous power. We always co-create with others. We participate in relationships, all kinds of relationships: career, partnerships in business, in love and with family.

Sometimes when we are faced with certain people who seem to be quite the opposite of us, either the Universe and Life are showing us how we are unique or there is a lesson for us to learn. The fact is, we always have choices in life, no matter how limited they seem. This is one of the most difficult realizations for us as human beings.

I remembered how a few years earlier I was faced with a difficult situation where I thought only two choices were available: A or B.

Neither seemed to be the best possible solution, and therefore I did not take any action. Instead I reflected and meditated on the subject for a few weeks and I realized there were so many other choices possible and available that I could not see before. My brain had already eliminated those possible available choices because I was operating in absolutes. This led me to a new discovery that other choices more suited to me were possible and I was free to choose any of them. In the process I also discovered that previous choices in life led me to face that particular situation. If in the past I had made every single choice aware of my intention, then different situations would have arisen and I would not have been in that position.

It was a discussion I vowed to have with this incredible group of women, knowing how much it would help. What is the intention behind our choice every single time we make a decision? At any moment we make a number of choices. What do I eat now? How do I spend my evening tonight? Do I return that phone call? Our choices and decisions have consequences. We may ask ourselves: Do I take this job because there is no other job out there? If we take the job because we feel we have no other choice, we can either think we are accepting a temporary setback or intentionally taking the position to provide for our family in the meantime and refuse to give up on our dreams. Fear and upset are replaced by hope and intent, where we make choices with power. The renewed energy can take us to higher vibrations and joy.

I looked at the clock: half past four in the afternoon. As much I wanted to say something I had no words. I sat there quietly while everyone chatted.

"Where is Georgina?" Mrs. Trevor suddenly asked.

At that moment, she entered the lounge with a panicked look, wearing a white robe, her hair wrapped in a white towel, and holding her phone.

"What's the matter?" Sarah asked.

"It's final. He was served with the separation papers," Georgina said.

"When? How?" Mrs. Trevor asked.

"Today. I didn't wanna tell you I kicked him out of the house a month ago. I got a good divorce lawyer."

"Where is he living?" Terri wanted to know.

"I dunno and I don't care. Probably with his bitch!" Georgina exclaimed. "We sent the papers to his work." She paused. "Imagine you have made a commitment to making a life with someone and it's ending right before your eyes." Georgina sighed. "The children's lives will be upside down, the emotional turmoil... We may have to move into a new home. What chaos."

Mrs. Trevor soothed. "The anxiety of money over relationship breakdown! It's a tough one."

"There are rules regarding division of assets in a marriage breakdown. We talked about this," Terri said with concern.

Georgina cried: "It's not just the money." She put both hands to her head. "What am I gonna do?" She started crying.

Mrs. Trevor turned to her. "Georgina, you will figure it out! We are all here for you."

I couldn't help but say: "I am glad you made your choice Georgina. The world is all about relationships. However we look at it, we are always dealing with people. By taking action you are controlling your own life and have power over what you do. If you cannot resolve the problem, eliminate the problem.

"The key is to take responsibility for our actions and feelings instead of blaming others or having negative emotions. Our emotional stability does not depend on our surroundings or the people we are involved with. We can be affected by others, but to be controlled by negative emotions is not healthy.

"One of my favorite concepts is to recognize the difference between a need, a want and a desire. For example you may need transportation to go from A to B. You can take public transport or a taxi or walk but you want a car. However you may desire a Ferrari or a Lamborghini.

"When it is a physical need, it may be the need for air, water, food, shelter or clothing. When there is an emotional need, a sense of time is involved."

Georgina looked curious, unsure whether hers was an emotional need or a physical need based on her emotional reaction to serving her husband with separation papers. It seemed to me she had an emotional need to be married and was also in fear for her financial needs, which are physical.

"My favorite is desire, which leads to hope and possibility," I shared with the group. "For example, if you desire a Ferrari or a Lamborghini it means you are hopeful, and you think it is possible for you to own it.

"The issue is when you think, 'I need this or that, or else.' That means you have an attachment to it, as if your self-esteem depends on it. We've got to distinguish between physical need, which is all about survival, and emotional need. We often mistake the two. When we are born we are completely helpless, and totally rely on adult support. Ultimately need is based on survival. However, as adults the question becomes what is it in that reality or that need that drives us to think about survival? The emotional need gets mistaken for a physical need and therefore we fall into survival mode.

"Another question is how to turn the need into a want. If there is nothing to participate joyfully from or with, we die. Participation is a form of engagement in life. That is why Emotional Resilience is effective.

"For example, Georgina, what is it you need emotionally from this marriage to survive? And if that thing is taken away can you survive?"

She looked at me as if puzzled.

"Also consider when you think you need to separate versus you want to separate. The emotional charge changes from negative to positive, leaving you in a more joyful state.

"One way to look at it would be through an action oriented affirmation such as: I want to feel _____ so I am going to do _____ ."

Sarah asked: "Do you think it is self-ish or self-less to separate with two children?"

I said: "How about self-in? That is, going after what you want, your passion, loving what you do for others and for yourself?"

I asked everyone if they would like some tea or refreshments to continue our discussion a little while longer and then go out for dinner on a positive note to celebrate life. They happily agreed.

"There are many ways to decrease anxiety and fear and increase confidence and hope. Since we don't have a lot of time today how about I just mention a few points?"

Terri took out her laptop. She said she could use the concepts for her team as well and would send the notes to everyone.

- Fear leads to reaction which leads to activity that is not the best
- The absolute of your memory is not the absolute of the situation
- New decisions modify your past
- Everything is temporary
- Testing your reality is your responsibility since it could be a cultural memory

- Modify your steps, taking a couple at a time up or five at a time down
- Test how when you are intentionally rude, you become less defensive
- Do not let your past dictate your future
- Your failures get overwhelmed by your successes
- Your unpleasant memories are overlaid by pleasant ones
- When you neutralize the absolute it is not an attack anymore and creativity can occur
- Neutralize the issue which leads to no fear
- Coping mechanisms; if you survived it, you have skills which are useful
- On the spiral of life any point along it becomes part of the experience
- If not familiar with a situation or feeling, if you experience something later you have to integrate it
- Everything is choice; yes, no, will go with the flow
- If you are intentional your life will be much more conductive; the way you want it
- I have control over my choices and how they affect me. Nothing is permanent

Mrs. Trevor said: "That is a lot for one day."

I smiled. "Everyone will gravitate towards one or a few of the concepts. Focus on what resonates with you."

Sarah stood up. "This is cool! I am taking three home. *Do not let your past dictate your future, Everything is temporary,* and *New decisions modify your past.* I like it!"

Nellie said: "I like *The absolute of your memory is not the absolute of the situation* and *Neutralize the issue which leads to no fear.*"

Terri exclaimed: "These are wonderful. *Everything is choice; yes, no, will go with the flow, Modify your steps, taking a couple at a time up or five at a time down* and *On the spiral of life any point along it becomes part of the experience.* We actually discussed this in our initial meetings."

I was truly pleased and delighted to see everyone taking a few points to work with.

Mrs. Trevor was not always easy to read; she was a wise and complicated woman. "At my age I have experienced successes, failures, triumphs and heartaches," she said, then paused to collect her thoughts and continued: "I can relate to *Coping mechanisms; if you survived it, you have skills which are useful, Your unpleasant memories are overlaid by pleasant ones* and *Your failures get overwhelmed by your successes.*" She stared into the distance again as she sometimes did.

Georgina said: "I am really thankful to have you all around me, especially at a time like this. It's really true that as women we help and support each other and confide in one another. But sometimes women are in competition, so it doesn't always work. We're a good team."

There was a sparkle in everybody's eyes.

I was filled with joy. " We have a strong bond between us. I felt it at the party and that for some reason we were all connected at a deeper level. Georgina, do any of the points mentioned resonate with you?" I asked.

"Oh yes. *Fear leads to reaction which leads to activity that is not the best, If you are intentional your life will be much more conductive; the way you want it,* and *I have control over my choices and how they affect me. Nothing is permanent.* I am going to remember these everyday as I go through this situation with my husband."

I thanked everyone for sharing. As much as I wanted to share my thoughts regarding the points we were discussing, I didn't want us to be late for our reservation at the city's most prestigious restaurant. We officially ended our day at the spa and headed out to Sarah's birthday dinner.

* * *

We were treated like royalty at the restaurant. We were all relaxed and glowing as we sat down by the window with the most breathtaking view of the city. This was our first time dining and celebrating together and our mood was exultant. Sarah looked smashing, talking, laughing; her beautiful, long shiny hair floating down over her shoulders while her eyes sparkled. We toasted to her twenty-first birthday, raising and clinking our glasses. The dinner menu looked heavenly. Considering all of the options, it was difficult to choose, but we finally ordered.

I was surprised when Nellie asked me to continue the conversation we left off at the spa. I asked if everyone would like to continue and they gave me a definite yes. I began: "I have been thinking about my lineage and culture for a while. I currently work with and explore the statement *Testing your reality is your responsibility since it could be a cultural memory*. I find it fascinating." I took a sip of my drink.

"Refreshing! And compelling," Mrs. Trevor said.

"I'm also interested *in When you neutralize the absolute it is not an attack anymore and creativity can occur*," I added.

"Please explain," Terri said.

"Let me first define the three areas of Rational Cognitive Awareness, which I identify as Interest, Concern and Attack.

When we are confronted with any subject matter, one of the best approaches is to identify whether the issue is: 1- of interest to you 2- of concern to you or 3 - you feel you are being attacked.

If something is of interest, it's not necessarily a concern. You can be strengthened by life when you are more interested than concerned. When you are interested you pay attention. If you pay attention long enough because you are interested you become concerned. The key is to change your perspective. Now because you are concerned that is when you expand.

"Even if I don't really understand what you're saying I'm loving this intellectual conversation," Sarah said, and laughed.

I burst out laughing too. "If you are in the area of interest is it an exciting interest? If you stay in the exciting interest you stay in joy. If not, what is the concern?"

"Sarah, are you interested in this subject because it's exciting? Or because you're concerned about what we're talking about?"

"It's exciting!" Sarah claimed.

"Great, otherwise my question would be, what are you concerned about? And my second question would be, does it concern you as well as society? Maybe parts and pieces of society will be harmed and that will affect you? That is when you think, I am being attacked."

"I get it," Sarah said. "Being excited about the subject is different than if I was interested in the subject matter because it was a concern, right?"

"Exactly! But let's say you are interested and it's because you feel attacked. We are talking about the statement *When you neutralize the absolute it is not an attack.* For example, you shared that you use drugs to calm yourself. What if I said drugs are used by people who have no resiliency skills? Now you take it as a direct attack. When you feel attacked is it a physical attack? If yes, respond to physical threat quickly. But you won't die if you feel attacked about other things such as money or a job. Stop doing nothing and do something; be in command of the event, of what is being attacked."

Sarah pondered and took a sip of her drink.

"Ask yourself how much control you really have. If you say I can't or I won't, is this mine? If it's other than mine, you may have to participate differently. What can you do differently? If you have not done it before, it's new and if it's new, it's joyful. Take control and be mindful of time and the event.

"For timing, ask yourself how long you have. What is it you are dealing with? If you have to respond quickly it might be a threat but if you respond reactively, how much time do you think you have? If a short time, then make the time as long as appropriate. The sooner you do something the sooner it goes away."

"So what you're saying is, do I take the subject matter personally? And do I feel attacked by that?" Sarah asked.

I nodded. "Then not to feel attacked you must do something different. When you are doing something you've never done before, expect mistakes as it won't be perfect right away. It can lead to How can I do it differently?, which then leads to curiosity. This is choosing deliberately! Refocus your what and reset your time to be surprised.

I asked them to think of these four elements:

1. What am I afraid of?
2. What is going to change? Deliberately take action.
3. What is threatened?
4. What is your expectation? Get up and do something.

"Is it ProCrastination or AmateurCrastination?" I asked.

Terri burst out laughing: "AmateurCrastination! I love it. That will be very useful at work."

We all chuckled. Then I offered another example.

"A common sense of purpose must have an element of co-operation. The intention of the agreement is fulfilled by usage like, I love us together. Agreements: Do you make them, or do you break them? As long as the other person does not lose, you can re-establish the agreement, which fulfills expectation.

"With the quality of discernment, allow yourself to be affected in order to be effective. When you are more discerning it can ignite more passion. The more discerning you are the more effective you are. The discernment quality of love is the glue that holds it all together."

Georgina asked Nellie to pass the salt, and then said: "Go on. We are listening."

"I know the subject matter maybe a little confusing so let me use myself as an example," I continued.

I was interested in writing this book. Once I started, I thought it was boring, so I stopped. But interest had ignited my passion, so I restarted writing. Then I was concerned: Is it good enough? I was afraid of being judged and not well received by readers; therefore, I felt emotionally attacked. I procrastinated for a long time which was not exactly intentional. After a while I restarted writing again. I discovered my messages were not coming through as intended. So I hired a book coach to guide me. In working with her I was encouraged to write differently, which led me to curiosity which in turn led me to explore and that expanded my creativity. Here I am."

Terri was thrilled. "I love it."

"Exploration brings joy. Joy is subjective. For example, if you are joyful because of your success then success breeds the confidence to take a risk," I continued.

"As we know, adrenalin can cause a temporary rush while reaching for success, or once we are at the pinnacle of success. Constantly running on adrenalin can be exhausting and harmful to the body. It can cause burnout. I have created a new word called Adaptine, which is the opposite of adrenalin. I love this word! Running on Adaptine means you are peaceful, joyful and yet passionate.

"To sum up, you start with interest, concern and then attack. When you feel attacked emotionally, doing things differently based on perceived time, agreements and discernment, leads to curiosity and ultimately exploration. Exploration, whether common or uncommon, leads to joy."

Mrs. Trevor's face lit up with every word.

"Highly passionate, sentient beings are cognizant, intelligent beings who are willing to participate and observe. Every day, every moment is a blank canvas. Somewhere on that canvas you can change something because it is humorous to you. You can change something in your mental picture.

"One way to play or to change is to see how many times a day you can participate in engagements where other people give up their absolutes. You don't force or teach this, just effectively entice an addition, more than one way of seeing things. When participating in these interactions, you must be emotionally honest and intellectually capable. You can learn how to shift and add a different reality."

"Yes, I agree. I always saw life in absolutes. It's either this or that; very black and white. I'm beginning to see the vast in between," Georgina expressed.

"We cannot reach our goals and aspirations by ourselves. We are in constant contact with the people around us," I continued. "When our vision is clear, many beings are instrumental in making our vision a reality. Therefore being able to work closely with people, to harness their insights and participation will help us fulfill our vision faster. Life is to be played with. As human beings we feel common ground when we understand instincts.

"We form an opinion right away when we meet someone, but when we speak to them again another time, we might see a different side of the same person that is opposite to what we first thought.

We can also acknowledge another person's opinion, that he or she sees something that way, but we don't have to see it that way ourselves.

We can acknowledge that we understand how he or she sees it that way. This realization can help us avoid being in a constant attack mode."

Mrs. Trevor and Terri simultaneously said: "Very accurate."

"Life is a dream," Mrs. Trevor said.

Sarah raised her glass cheerfully. "It sure is."

"Universal truths offer safety. If it does not work then it's a problem," I confirmed.

"What do you mean?" Nellie asked.

"Think of it this way: the sun rises every day, which is one universal truth. A sense of safety arises from knowing this truth. The dream comes when you accept what is, for what it is and not what it should be; meaning you must detach the picture from the absolute way in which you want to see your dream come true!"

"Does this mean I cannot dream about my absolute perfect dessert?" Terri asked.

At that exact moment the waiter brought us the dessert menu. I excused myself for a moment and spoke to him by the entrance, asking him to organize all the dessert orders and bring a cake for Sarah with twenty-one candles.

After my return I posed a question. "Is a joyful life a hopeful life?"

I looked around at delighted, smiling faces unsure of the answer.

"When you are joyful there is an element of lightheartedness and when you are hopeful it seems all things are possible. However, there is a correlation between joy and hope. Hope has a positive correlation with self-esteem, perceived problem-solving abilities, perception of control, optimism, positive affect and expecting positive outcomes.

175

When you are hopeful it means you believe in the future; as a result you speak to yourself in a positive way and in a positive voice that whatever it may be is possible. You may refer to your previous successes and experiences especially when you face challenges and remember how you handled them."

Then I posed another question. "Are you joyful because you are hopeful, or are you are hopeful because you are joyful?"

Terri asked: "How about both?"

"Very good question, Terri," I said. "High achievers are generally very positive and hopeful. I also find most people who are religious or spiritual are quite hopeful. In order to assess hopefulness you can think of how attainable or realistic your goal is."

I asked each person to assess their hopefulness based on the following:

- What is your attitude about it and how do you perceive your goal?
- What were the biggest challenges in reaching your goal?
- What emotions do these challenges elicit?
- Have you taken any steps to overcome the challenges?
- How do you feel about the outcome?

"One important element in order to achieve a state of joyfulness and or hopefulness is a sense of belonging," I addressed the group.

"I think that's true because I don't feel I belong anywhere," Sarah said.

Nellie responded quickly: "You belong here with us, Sarah."

We all smiled at her.

I continued: "A sense of belonging is one of the most important elements of well-being in human relationships. It has been studied that social isolation increases the risk of death about as much as smoking cigarettes and even more than either physical inactivity or obesity. As human beings we are social creatures and have a need to belong."

"Absolutely," Mrs. Trevor claimed.

"Belonging is a subjective state affected by our mood, health, and self-perception," I explained. "It has nothing to do with how many people you know or places you are associated with. The definition of belonging in psychology is a secure sense of fitting in. It is also a feeling of being taken in and accepted as part of a group. It relates to being approved of and accepted by society in general. In a unique community you can share goals, stay together, care for each other and help if needed."

Sarah and Georgina nodded.

"We all want a sense of belonging as human beings. At times you may participate in arts, sports, business, spiritual or religious groups. Although you may have common interest in the subject matter, you might feel you do not belong there, that you don't fit or don't connect with at least some of the people in that group. In order to feel you belong you might act differently or in a way that you think will make people like you or accept you. But to be your true self is to stay centered and real. The key is to feel that you belong."

Mrs. Trevor seemed quite interested in this subject. "Yes, I belong to a few different groups. My favorites are my Church group and our group."

Terri raised her glass. "Here's to us and to our celebration this evening."

We were all animated and raised our glasses.

"The second aspect to achieve a state of joyfulness and or hopefulness is to allow an element of surprise. That is, expect that unexpected things will happen. This can lead to discovery which in turn can lead to curiosity. It is in the state of curiosity that magic and creativity will occur and take us to a happier place."

The waiter arrived with a big cake accompanied by the other waitstaff singing Happy Birthday. We all joined in. Sarah looked so beautiful, glowing with happiness.

I said: "Make a wish before blowing out the candles."

She closed her eyes, took a big breath in and blew out all the candles with one breath. We celebrated, cheered and enjoyed the rest of the evening.

Chapter 6

Your Empowered Self

6

W e decided to accept Mrs. Trevor's cottage invitation a month later. It was only an hour and a half from the city. She said she would meet us there. I picked up everyone and drove to the countryside. Along the way, we reminisced about our wonderful spa day, and the breathtaking view and heavenly meal at the restaurant still lingered in our minds.

We arrived at the cottage on a lake. The scent of water and fresh air was soothing. The maid and her husband greeted us. They had set up comfortable chairs and arranged the table by the lake. A couple of luxury boats were moored at the private dock. A few chairs were set up on the beach, where you could sit and put your feet in the lake. Mrs. Trevor came and warmly welcomed us. It was peaceful to enjoy the moment, the serenity of nature. It was so tranquil, no one wanted to speak.

I excused myself and sat on one of the chairs near the water. It was a clear blue sky and the rays of the sun shone brightly on my face. After a few blissful moments I thought about human existence, the power of nature and our relationship to it.

After a few minutes they all came one by one and sat close soaking their feet in the majestic, healing waters.

"We are spiritual beings having a human experience in a human body. Despite being in charge of our lives and having choice we co-create with Spirit or Life. When we take a step towards our vision the Universe helps us to create that vision. We are not supposed to know the details of exactly how we will accomplish and manifest our vision, but to plan the steps and take inspired action towards them."

Terri, being a business strategist, was frowning in disagreement. "I don't get it, and I don't think that's true."

"Have you noticed whenever you made plans to do something they didn't turn out exactly the way you planned?" I asked. "If you have a clear vision and purpose, it will come to be but not the way you imagined it. That is because we are not supposed to know."

Terri gazed at the lake before she spoke. "Every time we implement our detailed business plan, something comes along to shift it. That's true. We always have to adapt, but the beauty is we sometimes achieve even better results!"

"That brings me to the concept of the One Third Universe." I looked around the group.

Mrs. Trevor's lips were pursed, her hands fidgeting. "I am a Christian and I believe in the Bible."

"Religion does not dismiss the Universe and talks about faith, correct?" I asked.

She nodded.

"I am not telling it much differently. Based on ancient wisdom and Universal Principles we are one third in the universe; everything we do and are is expressed by one third of us and the other two thirds by the world outside of us. This is the Law of Isness that affects everything in the Isness. If you don't add your one third there would be a sense of anxiety.

"For example, if you picture what you want, you can make it happen by the one third you are capable of; the other two thirds of the picture will not come from you.

"Take a look at our gathering today; did you know exactly what we were going to do and say?"

"Interesting, go on," Mrs. Trevor said.

To my surprise Terri leaned in with curiosity.

I continued. "Pay attention to the things you do know; which is you. We are three-dimensional beings on earth: height, weight and depth. We can get to five dimensions which include time and space (spatial reality). The fourth part is lack of awareness. Knowing you have the ability to reach five dimensions, moving the unknown to known is grace. Be an active participant in knowing yourself. You can have the grace to understand that you don't like not knowing. What you don't know, won't hurt you! There is predictability, projection, acceptance and discovery; move the unknowable unknown to knowable unknown. When you have a purpose, which is one third, the other two thirds will step in and help. For example, my purpose is serving; therefore there is joy and less frustration. As a result when I say, 'I will' the Universe will aid that."

"When I was little I used to know things," Sarah said in a quiet voice. "I could see and hear things that were not in actual reality. I could feel other people."

Georgina shouted with excitement; "So you are an intuitive and an empath!"

Nellie had an enchanted look on her face while Terri looked puzzled.

"Sarah, I'd love to hear more about that," I said.

She continued: "I remember one time I heard a voice in my head that said, 'Go see your grandpa.' I thought, why would I want to do that? I couldn't go by myself anyways, so I ignored it. The voice kept saying, 'You've got to go.' So I asked my mom if we could go. She said OK and we did. When we arrived, we knocked on the door but there was no answer. We knocked a few more times, still no answer. But we could hear some noise. My mom turned the knob, and the door was open. When we went in, Grandpa was lying on the floor, no one was home and the radio was on."

We were all quiet, listening to every word.

"My mom called emergency right away. Paramedics came and took Grandpa to the hospital. Later they told us he had had a stroke and would've died if we hadn't arrived in time."

"Unbelievable!" Terri exclaimed.

Sarah continued: "When I was seven I dreamed that I had a beautiful baby girl with blond hair, but she didn't have a daddy." She teared up. "And another time my daddy's coworker came to our home. He looked weird. I thought, 'he's gonna steal something.' I felt my father was anxious, but I didn't know why. A few days later my mom's only diamond necklace, an inheritance from her great-grandmother, was missing. After feeling all these things for a while, I told my parents, but they punished me and told me never to think about these things or talk to anyone about them. I think I blocked it, so I don't feel."

"Sarah, Universe was telling you something, helping you access information. Why don't you embrace your powers and Inner Wisdom, especially since your accuracy is so high?" I asked.

Nellie and Georgina agreed.

Sarah smiled shyly. "I like that."

I continued: "One third we are responsible; two thirds can be creative and magic. There is freedom in that. Understanding that you feel self-doubt draws a sense of doubt and two thirds of the Universe will push you towards a greater awareness and movement that it is all right not to know. If you don't know but need to know it will be brought in by the Universe.

"It's good for you to doubt that you have an effect because that leads you to do something.

"The projected idea of someone doing something is rarely accurate, therefore a sense of wonder leads to excitement. The thought that it's all yours isn't true. You have an effect, but you don't know what it is. One third affects the Universe so much more than you think it does. Own your effect with purpose, and intention, claim it! The more you put into life, the more life will put into you. Trying to control the two thirds leads to frustration and discomfort. Therefore it's not really all yours. Universe balances things out."

"So let me see if I understand you correctly," Terri began. "Even when I plan my business strategies and think I am fully in charge it still represents one third of the equation?" She paused and I nodded. "And the two thirds can be creative and magic if I let it be by simply having a clear purpose and intention and claim my vision?"

"Yes. As long as you are not at cross purposes you can co-create. Raw energy will be available; Universe will help with that sense of purpose. Do the most unpredictable thing, which is the most creative thing. Take a chance and do it differently. Play with life!"

"I am amazed," Terri said. "I think looking at everything with this perspective will reduce fear and anxiety, especially at work."

I dabbled my feet in the water with joy. "To not be harmed by what you don't know, pay attention to what you do know, which is one third. Creating draws co-operation; Universe will provide whatever is necessary for the greatest good which leads to a greater sense of joy."

"You can tune in to Universe by accepting what is, which in turn allows introspection, and not because it is broken. That gets you moving along, taking charge of something that is yours."

"Any bit of change is useful because it involves exciting participation," I revealed. "Sometimes you don't recognize the

Universe's co-operation. Anything you do because you choose to do it, changes you. Hope lives at the point where you participate.

"Explore! You have unique strengths; try to express them more often. In meditation the one third that is you connects you to the ten-dimensional you.

The rule of the Universe is three: past, present and future or beginning, middle and end. You cannot divide something by three; it is a never-ending continuance. One third is whole; dividing it by three results in infinity."

Mrs. Trevor pulled her feet out of the water and got up slowly. "I must say I have learned new concepts which are a bit hard to digest based on my previous ideas and thought processes. However, I will make an effort to incorporate them into my daily living. Having said that, what do you think of having some lunch?"

We all gathered in the shade, grateful for some relief from the hot sun and the refreshing lunch.

I looked at everyone as they ate quietly and noticed they all looked more vibrant compared to the first time we met a few months earlier, more expanded and at peace.

After lunch, settled in our comfortable chairs, I asked if anyone wanted to talk about a specific subject. Terri said she had been reading and wondering about power versus empowerment.

"Power is the authority to act and Empowerment is the permission to act!" I began. "Think about it for a moment. What would be an example of authority to act? A CEO of a company has authority to act, to make changes to put certain policies in place. A king or a queen of a country has authority to act."

Terri was intrigued and blinked eagerly for me to continue.

"Empowerment is permission to act. I am referring to permission that comes from within, although permission can be given from an employer to employee, or permission given to certain individuals for certain opportunities in some communities or groups.

"An empowered person has more control over his or her life, can make decisions independently and most importantly can come from a place of choice. When we intentionally make choices that come from our heart because we desire something or because of strategic thinking, we are in charge. We take full responsibility for our choices, decisions and as a result the consequences." I paused. "Now would you rather be in power or be empowered? Or perhaps both?"

Sarah jumped up, raised her arms in the air and burst out: "Yes, yes. I wanted to tell you guys, but I was waiting for the right moment. I gave up drugs. I guess I am empowered now, right?"

We all jumped up, hugged and congratulated her. I was thrilled to see her progress. What a beautiful soul Sarah was. When I met her, she came across as bitter and harsh, yet I could see inside that exterior she was so fragile and weak that I would have loved to just step in and rescue her.

"Sarah," I said as we returned to our seats. "I am truly delighted to celebrate you, who you are and who you have become. I am sure it wasn't easy to do what you did."

"I'd like to know what brought about the change, Sarah," Mrs. Trevor asked.

Sarah was beaming, and for the first time I saw her as a woman instead of a timid young girl.

"Well, your support and love meant a lot to me, and still does. All the stuff we have discussed about choice, mindset and how we can change our lives combined with the fact that I was scared I wouldn't see Anusha grow up made me think I could do it. So I did with full power." Then she looked at me and said: "You love that right, the power stuff?" She winked at me with the most vibrant smile.

I started laughing and before I knew it, everybody else did too. It was a perfect moment.

"Moment by moment we build life, the decisions we make every moment have an impact, an effect on our lives.

"To give away your power is to give away your strength," I said to this marvelous group. "You can misuse your power, be overpowered or be powerless. The idea here is to realize what kind of power you are experiencing and make an effort to stay empowered.

"If you seek power, what kind of power and for what reason? When it comes to business and money, you must give yourself permission that it is OK to have wealth and it is OK to be successful. How much money do you want? And why do you want it? When you know why, it is easier to reach your goal.

"Many people want more wealth thinking it adds to their power. Money does not define you! But it gets you closer to your financial goals. What do you want to do with the money? How much wealth do you want to create? Are you creating wealth to be in power or to be empowered? You can magnify your power by having the ability to do what you want and have the permission within yourself to do what you want. On the other hand, you may seek political power to make lasting change for the good of humanity versus power to control and manipulate. Remember be aware and know you always have a choice!"

"I am truly fascinated," Mrs. Trevor said.

"I know the games being played at work regarding power," Terri added. "In my position I need to play their game."

"It depends on your desires, Terri. If you are playing the game because you feel you don't have a choice, you are actually giving away your power," I added.

Terri closed her eyes for a moment, pensive.

A light breeze covered my face. "Living consciously is empowering knowing you always have a choice in all that you do. You can live your life with peace and passion and create a fulfilling life. If you do not make decisions and take actions for yourself, life will, and sometimes that can work against you."

Georgina had been quiet all afternoon, paying attention and taking notes. She looked up at me. "So these concepts seem a bit ambiguous, but I think I understand them on a deeper level even if I can't articulate it well. What I understand is that we need to be aware of our choices, why we make them, what we get because of those choices and above all, if we make them based on fear then we're not gonna be happy, right?"

Nellie confirmed that emphatically. "Exactly, and that's why our choices must be aligned with our purpose."

"Your sense of purpose comes from your passion, which creates oxytocin, the feel-good chemicals that are released similar to when you laugh, are tickled or bond with someone. When you use Will and Power, remember the third energy center in co-operation, it is good. However, if you are fearful you give up will and power. You can amplify using will and power or discernment. Take a piece of knowledge that you have and repurpose it," I added.

A handsome man was walking towards us with a smile. Mrs. Trevor introduced him as her eldest son Jack. Jack said Mrs. Trevor talked about us often and he was curious to meet us. He offered to take us for a ride on the yacht. The women's faces filled with joy at the thought of spending an hour on that opulent yacht on sparkling waters. I thought it would be wonderful for body, mind and spirit.

The yacht was magnificent. It had four cabins, a living room with a bar, and a huge open space on the main floor with beautifully designed, comfortable wicker chairs around a big rectangular table secured to the floor.

"This is gorgeous," I complimented Jack.

"Yes, it's the family yacht and we love it. As a big family, we take turns using it for our own individual families."

"The best is when we are all together, with all my children and grandchildren." Mrs. Trevor lit up.

I sat on a comfortable leather chair and felt pure joy and bliss, looking out at the water, the sun, and the blue sky. I felt one with the Universe and kept giving gratitude for a beautiful life. My thoughts were on the moment and the moment only; the sound of splashing water, taking in the fresh air and the beauty of nature. I was absorbed and totally immersed but could hear laughter as everyone else was talking and laughing.

After about an hour and a half, we came back to land. Nellie seemed utterly relaxed and Georgina told us the ride was truly good for her soul.

"Our existence is in ourselves; within our Isness," I returned to the topic from earlier. "The only thing we can't escape is our body, borrowed from the earth and to be returned to the earth. To be enlightened is to live in the light; to be adaptable, flexible and expressive which leads to joy. When you can ground a metaphysical idea, more neuropathways open up in your brain and you will have access to more ideas. Get relaxed and get creative!"

"I am starting to be very interested in this," Terri admitted.

Nellie shared that she loved the metaphysical and had been reading about it for some time.

"The more you become aware of who you truly are, the more enlightened you become," I said. "The key is to see the truth of you without criticizing."

"'Know thyself' right? Isn't that what you told us in the beginning?" Sarah said.

"Exactly! We often think of ourselves only as conscious beings. Let's explore a little further. We refer to three levels: conscious, subconscious and unconscious.

"Unconscious is raw stimulus. Subconscious is stimulus that drives the conscious mind, a gate keeper, a cellular over structure. This is where everything about yourself has been recorded. The conscious mind sits on top of that.

"The unconscious mind tries to confirm your past which is not necessarily now. It tries to create that which it has not seen before. Nothing is absolute. Everything is in transition. So the environment in your life is there to be seen differently, to get the greatest good from it. Every moment in life is valuable. In your past, even every guilty moment was gold and is valuable, but you did not see the value of it."

I looked around at the sparkling eyes. "We all have something of value! The light within us is necessary!"

I felt a sense of humility engulfing the air.

"Your soul enters the Universe with the intention to observe for the timeframe it lives in the body. As an enlightened person you understand you have the exact choices you need in front of you. Awareness is the ability to separate what is yours and what is not yours. Gossip for example; any aspect of any observation of any other human being. Are you with me so far?"

"I think I feel what you are saying more than I know it logically," Sarah said.

"In order to feel empowered attempt to embody all aspects of life. To do that we must know about the three levels I just described. Our spirit or soul is here to observe all of our creation without judgement.

Our subconscious mind records all that has ever happened in our lives and our conscious mind tries to understand it with limited knowledge. The idea is to tap into our subconscious mind and glimpse our unconscious mind, which we can access with regular meditation. By understanding how they work and how they are related we increase joy."

"This will take a lot of time!" Sarah looked at everyone.

"Yes, and there are many parts to it. Ultimately as human beings we want to increase joy. Being empowered adds to joy. I am sharing some parts, so you understand and know how we operate on a core level, which includes the totality of our being. Think of these three primal elements: 1. Instinct 2. Consistency and 3. Exploration.

"Instincts are there to protect. They are for your survival. Consistency brings safety and once you feel safe exploration can begin. Most people are stuck in survival mode.

"It is predicted consistency. Unexpected consistency against our instincts could be viewed as life being interesting. The process of exploration leads to more joy. Fear and defensiveness are not exploration."

Terri asked if I could give an example.

"Call an unsuspecting friend, a relative or a stranger and do something different, something that violates your consistency, and see what happens. Or take the example of a business that calls you at dinner time. Find the director of that company and call them at meal-time. Or if a telemarketing person calls, deliberately tie them up so they can't call anybody else. Play with it."

Terri chuckled. "This is funny."

"This act increases your power of choice which decreases your fear," I explained. "This is one way to rise above self-defense. Consistency of new knowledge versus old reactive knowledge. Do it differently. The soul wants joy. Think about things in a different way by violating your consistency. This is a powerful technique." I paused and saw a mischievous expression on Sarah's face, slight worry on Mrs. Trevor's.

I took a few sips of the cold water in my glass.

"If you are uncomfortable about a decision it's because your mind has the wrong answer, but your subconscious and your unconscious have the answer. Otherwise you would not feel uncomfortable. The subconscious and unconscious mind are instinctively hiding you from lions. At your leisure, you can make the decision that is most joyful. Do something different.

"The conscious mind always goes along for the ride; the subconscious is instinct. In order, we have self-preservation, consistency and exploration, which is discovery. Do the things that are yours to do. Failure is also expansion!

"If you want a dream, you can change how it affects you. If you don't like it, do something about it. Life is a dream. Integrate something. Dream into a pleasant exertion. You can explore and that can be joyful.

"Do the unpredictable thing that creates chaos. You want to be attracted to the creative part of chaos not the distractive part of chaos. If something disturbs you, chaos can be created too. Your passion takes you beyond your belief. Leave 'Yes but' behind and let passion drive you. There is an opportunity to expand, express and create. Passion attracts more passion."

"I am loving this," Nellie shouted. "Use your instincts for survival, do things differently by interrupting your consistency and explore in order to increase your joy. Voila!"

"How about my situation?" Georgina asked. "My separation is official, and I have no idea what I'm supposed to do."

"Fear is survival based. True agreements are not based on your fear or the other person's. If fearful about something, stop the fear. Fight fear with feast," I responded.

"In any agreement, if the other side gets more than they expect, if they get more benefit, then they can participate more. Don't project that you want something and the only way to get it is if they give it to you. It is easy to ignore the other's fear. The value you receive is more than what you expend, therefore eliminate fear.

Georgina nodded.

"In relationships, you always argue about your benefit. Both parties are right because of the different pictures they both hold. You say, I have consistency and I am going to explore so I know I am right. Ask if there is any other way you can explore and you will get more answers. The art is to observe the other person and see from their point of view.

"You can get magic out of life when there is common purpose, and you have self-discernment. If you argue, argue relevance not that you are right. Your passion can't be shared by others. The reward is yours; it belongs to you. They may feel your passion, but it is not shared."

"If you are in fear, the art is just to ask the question to find out the answer even if you're afraid to hear. If you hear no problem, it means they don't understand it and don't trust it. If the answer is pure joy and pleasure, wait for six months. Six months after the issue will have changed. Make agreements every six months. It takes that long for consistency. As humans we are capable of disguising ourselves for six months. This has to do with the seasons. We can't hold the mask for more than six months."

Mrs. Trevor turned to Georgina: "Make decisions to reflect what you would like to see in your life and go for it without fear. Trust that the best will happen. By now you have a few valuable tools you can use."

Georgina nodded with a determined look then sipped her lemonade.

"Your past tells you defensively what is possible. Regenerate your sense of passion. Escape the faulty attempt. Fake it until you are it, not until you make it," I added.

"Explore what might be, not what should be. Be something entirely different than what you are. For one moment take away from the consistency of who you are and what you are, and see what happens."

"I understand." Georgina took a breath. "I've always seen myself in a certain way and behaved in a certain manner with my husband. I'm going to do things differently."

"To put it another way," I continued, "if you are in a sleeping bag and a rock is underneath you, you move the rock but then there is a hole, and you are uncomfortable again. Know that you had a hand in it. What you do with it provides you with unlimited resources. You can move every rock downhill or sleep somewhere else or whatever else you decide to do. Knowledge overcomes fear. There is fear of losing consistency. By violating consistency you expand, gain knowledge and, once that is consistent, you can explore.

"By violating your consistency you're adding to your self-control, which becomes a habit. The point of self-control comes from the passion to want to change or do something. It has the greatest effect on you, and not on anyone else, because you remember the emotion of it. Assume the effect you have on yourself, be gentle and helpful to yourself."

Sarah tilted her head. "So I violated my consistency of doing drugs without fear, which will help me with my exploration?"

Georgina shouted bingo!

My heart filled with joy to witness Sarah's moment of realization. "And Sarah, the exploration of yourself starts as you discover more about yourself. Express, expose and expand to find joy. Passion does not live in consistency but on both ends of survival and exploration. Being enlightened is knowing whatever it is, is yours and it becomes easy to explore, you are not fooled by yourself. Stake your claim to the point of reality is how I like to call it or declare your realizations."

Mrs. Trevor asked if we would like to pause for a barbeque dinner. We sat there enjoying the breeze and the sound of light waves while dinner was prepared. It was magical.

When we gathered around the table to eat, I turned to Mrs. Trevor. "I really appreciate all you have done for us today." When I raised my glass, everyone else did too. "To your courage in life! You have endured a lot of losses and yet kept your passion and have been able to maintain a very successful business."

We clinked glasses and sipped.

"Where do you get your courage?" I asked her.

"Courage is one of the most important virtues in life. As women we have a lot of inner strength. Our intuition and creative qualities are inherent. The mere fact that we are capable of giving birth is a creative process. When facing the worst situation, we just pull ourselves together and do whatever is necessary. Perhaps it is the survival instinct!"

"I wonder why we can't put this kind of strength and courage towards our goals and dreams all the time. What stops us?" I asked. "Is it negative beliefs about ourselves that we're not even aware of or is it much deeper than that?"

"My husband Gabby channeled all his grief and energy into the business; that is how we started. As for me, frankly I feared that if I didn't focus and keep the family together we might lose everything. We had children to look after. I became more involved in the business as time passed and once we were comfortable I didn't think much about fear. I was operating out of desire, as you called it. I had courage because I didn't feel fear."

"I believe some of us are naturally courageous and some may need guidance to build courage," I commented.

"How do you cultivate courage?" Nellie asked.

"I trust that the more authentic we are the more courageous we are. As discussed in our last talk it's the fear of not being accepted or being judged by others that causes us to not express who we truly are. By embracing our true self, we can take steps to increase our courage and go through life with more courage and less fear."

"Yes that is the answer I have found, to be true to myself," Terri shared. "It increases my courage to be a visionary."

"Absolutely," I agreed, "you need to be aware and make a conscious effort. Courage is a powerful thing! Life is like a big canvas. I always ask what you choose to draw on it. What color would you like to paint on it? Who is in your picture?"

Nellie smiled. "That is what I say: What do you choose to draw?" We all looked at her inquiringly. "I paint. I paint in vibrant colors, and I used to make sculptures."

"That's fantastic," Terri said: "When is your next art show? Is your work in a gallery?"

Nellie blushed. "Not anymore but I will exhibit again soon." Then she turned to me and asked me to please continue.

"I love that you express yourself through art, Nellie.

"Mindset is critical to quality of life. Mindset is a set of beliefs or a way of thinking that determines your behavior, outlook and mental attitude. There are two types of Mindsets: Fixed and Growth.

"Let's compare these two types. If you have a Fixed Mindset, most likely you have a desire to look smart and therefore would have a tendency to avoid challenges. Whereas if you have a Growth Mindset you have a desire to learn and therefore you would have a tendency to embrace challenges. When it comes to obstacles, if you have a Fixed Mindset, you will give up easily. If you have a Growth Mindset you will persist in the face of obstacles.

"As a Fixed Mindset person you see making an effort as fruitless or worse, and as a Growth Mindset person, you see effort as the path to mastery. Again if you have a Fixed Mindset, when it comes to criticism you will ignore useful negative feedback but if you have a Growth Mindset you learn from criticism. And in the last example if you have a Fixed Mindset you feel threatened by others' success and if you have a Growth Mindset you find lessons and inspiration in others' success."

"It's obvious, Mrs. Trevor and Terri, that you both have growth mindsets," Sarah said. "It's interesting how that plays a role in our lives."

I smiled and continued. "Another element that can increase empowerment is Your Spoken Words. Your words have power! Speak your truth, speak your heart's desires. Speak of your dreams and inspirations as life unfolds right before you.

"We humans are vibrational beings, and our thoughts and words have vibrational frequencies. Each of us vibrates at a certain energy level. Whatever your energy is attracts the same vibrational frequency, though it could be the opposite. If it is the same frequency and positive, it grows even bigger and creates momentum.

"The higher our vibrations the higher our power. Imagine a time where someone spoke to you with power and conviction and had a profound effect on you. What was it about the words that got your attention? When you speak with conviction you are aligned with who you truly are, and your words make more of an impact.

"Now how do you speak to yourself? Are you kind and gentle or do you constantly criticize yourself and expect yourself to do more and be more? If the latter, is it your voice or the voice of a parent or someone who influenced you?"

Sarah sniffed. "I remember my parents yelling: You will never amount to anything! Who do you think you are? I was so hurt but I believed it. I didn't think there was any hope for me or even a different possibility until our gatherings."

Nellie placed her arm around Sarah's shoulder and expressed how delightful she was to hear that, and we all agreed.

"When you speak to yourself with love and compassion you will be in a better emotional state," I said. "When you extend the same love and compassion to others you will have more impact than you can ever imagine.

"Did you know, at the beginning of time when humanity was created, we communicated telepathically, no words were exchanged? But as we evolved, we used language to express ourselves. However, as much as we have a common understanding of the words we use, words can have a different emotional connotation for different people. For example, if I say imagine a beautiful, tranquil place in nature where you feel a total sense of equanimity and serenity, I will get a few different responses as to what that looks like, and I used the same words."

"Yes," Terri chimed in. "Miscommunication can happen in business and personal relationships merely because the words have a different impact on different people, or simply because the feelings or thoughts were not expressed as intended. I always encourage my team to express themselves with words and make sure the person they are communicating with receives their true message."

"Tone of voice, body language and delivery of the message play an important role too," Georgina offered.

"Of course. This is my favorite," I said. "Do you tell yourself, I have this goal and I'll see if I can get it. Or do you say, I have a vision and I am inspired to work towards it and make my dream come to life?"

"Are your words positive or negative?"

Georgina's eyes lit up. "Yes I am inspired to make my dreams come true!"

We raised our glasses again. The maid cleared the table and we leaned back, pulling sweaters and shawls around our shoulders as the night air cooled. There was one last concept I wanted to discuss.

"To be truly empowered you must be the Authentic YOU. The true you! Your voice matters!"

"We are all bombarded by messages to be more successful, wealthier, thinner, prettier, sexier and the list goes on," Nellie complained.

"Yes. If you were to stop and think about exactly what you want out of life, what you want to accomplish and how much time and energy you are willing to allocate to it, instead of merely following everyone else, the world would be a happier place. The key is to pursue your own passion and your own path. You have a unique combination of energy, wisdom, intellect, influence, and experience that cannot be matched by anyone else."

"You might be one person in the world, or you might be the world to one person," Sarah said.

Georgina said she loved that.

"Embrace your uniqueness!" I implored them. "Everyone else is taken.

"Once you know your passion and your purpose, share it with the world. Surround yourself with people who believe in you and want to be around you. Go where you are celebrated instead of being tolerated! Keep smiling and the world will smile back at you. Say yes to your better version of yourself. When you are true to yourself the world benefits. When you follow your heart, you operate at higher vibrational energies and therefore shine brighter.

"Someone looking from the outside would never know your true desires and your destiny. They would only see you, and what and how you put it out in the world. What is it that you put out? Is it your true Authentic Self? Who are you really and who do you want to be? Who do you aspire to be? Or are you molded and shaped by your belief system that follows the social norms, social rules, and protocols?"

"You mean really be open?" Georgina asked. "That's not easy."

I agreed.

"Have you ever thought that an idea you have can change something for the better?" Terri rubbed her forehead, as if perplexed. "Say some procedure at work or a way of communication that could save time, or a project that could bring wonders to the world? What stops you from implementing it? Is it fear of people not accepting your solution or idea? Is it lack of courage? Are your negative thoughts and self-esteem holding you back? I am curious. Your feedback will be useful in my work."

"In your example I'd be afraid of being rejected," Georgina said. "And I wouldn't want my boss to think that I'm ready to take over his job."

"What if your ideas saved the company a lot of money? And because of your brilliance you were promoted to a much higher position?" Mrs. Trevor asked.

Georgina agreed. "True."

"The world needs you," I continued. "Speak up, implement your ideas, share your enthusiasm, tell the world that you are participating fully and are excited about it.

"Your voice matters. Express yourself. Speak about your desires, your dreams, your convictions, and your beliefs. Speaking and expressing can create a sense of harmony, a sense of release and a sense of belonging.

"When a butterfly flaps its wings, it can create wind in a different country, far from where the butterfly is. This is the ripple effect and it's important to know that you also have an effect. You may not express yourself because you think: What's the use? Nothing will change, or the other person may not even be interested in what I have to say.

"Always remember you have three times more impact than you think you have. Embrace your Authentic Self. The world needs you! Yes, the world needs you. The benefit is that you will also be more fulfilled, and the worst that can happen is that you will be closer to what you want. You may fear that others might judge you, so you do not want to risk it!

"Believe that what matters most is you!"

"Thank you," Terri said. "You've given me a different perspective and the courage to do something really bold at work."

It was late by now, and although Mrs. Trevor offered that we could stay overnight, we thanked her and piled into the car to return home to the city.

Chapter 7

Your Relationship with Money

7

Weeks passed. I could still remember the joy of being on the yacht, feeling the breeze, the sun on my face and the splashing sound of the water lingered in my whole being. I felt content without needing to do anything or be anywhere. Everyone was busy taking care of what they needed to and exploring the new concepts we had discussed.

Two months later I received calls and e-mails that it was time to get together again. I wanted to do something interesting, so I asked everyone to be prepared for an adventure and to wear something comfortable. I was excited to bring in some Egyptian Pharaonic statues, costuming and jewelry. I decorated the house with Pharaonic artifacts and added some see-through light colored-chiffon veils. You should have seen their faces when they entered the house. Georgina was thrilled, Mrs. Trevor was surprised, and Sarah wondered what era and country it was all from.

I welcomed everyone and explained about the Pharaohs who lived in Egypt a few thousand years ago. Everyone sat mesmerized. I put different head pieces and necklaces on them, including some long wrist and arm cuffs. Terri said she loved it.

I asked if anyone had experienced anything similar. They all said no. Then I asked if they knew what Emotional Profit was. Although they came up with some reasonable, logical explanations based on the words, the subject needed further clarification. So, I posed the question: If you had an opportunity to experience this exhilarated feeling of being transported to a different time and a different frame of mind, would you pay for it despite your limited budget?

Nellie mused: "It would be an interesting experience."

"I would!" Terri exclaimed. "Although I am careful with my money."

Mrs. Trevor looked pensive. The most interesting thing happened. She sat straight with her beautiful headpiece, leaned back, put her arms on the armrests and spoke like a Goddess: "I am what I am because I choose to be!"

Mrs. Trevor was about 5'2", with silver hair and glasses. But she looked much taller with her headpiece on, her erect posture and no glasses on. Then she snapped out of it and looked straight at me.

"I would definitely want the experience."

"Emotional Profit is a profit that drives us emotionally," I explained. "We all think we want money and wealth because it will give us a feeling of security, serenity, and peace of mind, a sense of accomplishment or a sense of power. Emotional Profit is about how it makes us feel. Emotional Profit is what gives us a feeling of joy, a feeling of enchantment and happiness without guilt.

"We may choose a behavior or a habit that goes against logic when it comes to money but choose to go ahead anyway after considering all aspects of the decision, because it makes us feel better. Creating and enjoying Emotional Profit can turn guilty spending into soul-enriching experiences."

Georgina laughed. "I have so many bills right now with my separation I couldn't even think about a luxurious experience like this."

"I know what you mean," Sarah agreed.

I continued. "Here is one example that can be used at a certain or appropriate time in your life. Let's say you have budgeted $5,000 for a trip this year but an opportunity has presented itself for the whole family to reunite by going on a trip to a particular destination: a family reunion. Let's also say that costs $8,000. Now you think, well that's

$3,000 more than what you budgeted. The decision then becomes about spending an extra $3,000 knowing your parents, children, aunts, uncles, cousins and other family members will be there. Who knows when you will get together again? If you have a deep desire to see everyone and it gives you joy, you may think you can cut your spending from other expenditures or not go on another trip for a year or two and take this special trip to see everyone. The $3,000 is one example of Emotional Profit because it can offer so much more pleasure and happiness."

Sarah said she loved that example. Mrs. Trevor sat deep in thought and shared how she was wondering if she might have taken a trip to experience what she was experiencing at that moment.

"I now understand the relationship between spending money for a joyous experience versus spending it just because you like something like a designer purse." Nellie thanked me.

Georgina said: "I like the family reunion example. I guess if we are aware of the extent of the emotional profit and our level of desire, we can choose wisely."

"Precisely." I was so happy my small simulation of an experience had the desired effect.

"I have a lot of wealth and can do practically anything I wish, but I feel different. I have never felt like this before even with all of my experiences," Mrs. Trevor shared.

"Power is the ability to act and Empowerment is permission to act," I repeated. "Mrs. Trevor, you have the power to buy or do anything, however you have given yourself permission to experience the joy of being a Goddess. Power and Empowerment are two different feelings. The empowered feeling or state is an inner strength and ability to experience joy. Power is not always associated with joy."

Mrs. Trevor and Terri said it made sense, while Sarah played with her arm cuffs and Georgina admired her necklace.

"Power comes in many forms and power of intent is the driving force. It is the intensity of your intent that makes things happen. Have you ever experienced a situation where you really wanted a chair or a piece of clothing or some item and you couldn't afford it but somehow you received money from an unexpected source, just enough to buy the item? Or you got it as a gift? Isn't that interesting?

"I remember when I was a student and on an extremely low budget I saw a beautiful black velvet dress on a manikin when I passed a boutique on my way to school. I definitely couldn't afford it and there was no way I was going to buy it. However, I admired the dress for days and days and imagined owning it every time I saw it. In my imagination I wore it to a party one evening surrounded by friends and everyone complimented me on the unique style. Soon after, I was delighted to see that the dress was on sale, fifty percent off! This exclusive boutique never put anything on sale for more than ten percent. I immediately purchased the dress because the price and the Emotional Profit were satisfying. This is an example of power of intent, desire and taking action."

Sarah giggled with joy. "Can I use similar things to bring money into my life? Like imagining I have a full-time job or even that I am studying at university?"

"Absolutely," I responded. "You can actively visualize an outcome and the process (though that's not always necessary) including details, feelings and excitement. Visualization or mental simulation is the experience of imagining. Your mind does not know the difference between reality and imagery because the same part of the brain is activated. The intense and powerful energy exuded during a meditation can have a penetrating effect on manifesting your desired outcome faster.

"If you are serious about what you want, take steps and inspired action towards it and look for opportunities. When you take a step, Universe rushes in to help you."

Mrs. Trevor admired her necklace and Terri marveled at Nellie's headpiece while listening.

I continued. "The motivation behind what we do is key. I believe motivation is derived from outside sources and inspiration: in Spirit is an internal drive, hence much more powerful. For example if your purpose is to have joy and your intention is to accumulate wealth, by taking steps you will fulfill the intention which will give you a sense of empowerment. When you state your short or long-term goal, you will need to check your internal mental dialogue and assess whether your thoughts are congruent with your inspiration.

"Profit is not just money. It could be passion. Passion attracts profit. What that profit is, is up to you. Profit presupposes something and you gain profit in some form."

Georgina secured her headpiece and walked around while showing off her pharaonic jewelry. We all burst out laughing and decided to have some exotic refreshments that I had prepared.

Nellie asked why I had all these soft veils, Egyptian artifacts, costumes and jewelry. I was delighted she asked as I love these things. I shared that I had collected them, buying or having them made for some of our dance theater productions.

After our break I posed another question: "How is your relationship with money?

"My relationship with money? Isn't that odd?" Terri asked.

"No," I responded, "because everything is a relationship! Your relationship with your money can be looked at in various ways. How do you treat your money? Are you generous with your money and buy what you desire most of the time? Are you frugal? Do you lend money to others if they ask? Do you waste money on things that don't offer returns or fulfillment?"

"I've lent money a few times. I am still waiting to get it back," Georgina grumbled.

Terri shook her head. "I never lend and never borrow!"

"I never had money to be generous." Disappointment traveled across Sarah's face.

Mrs. Trevor smiled at her. "Being generous has nothing to do with how much money you have."

Georgina nodded with certainty.

"There's another part to this. Do you have your own rules and ethics about how you will earn your money? Will you take any job to survive? Will you invest anywhere to make a return? Or you are very specific? When you decide how you earn your money and where to spend it or invest it you have a certain relationship with money that is near and dear to you. When you have answers to all these personal questions, then you have a better understanding of your relationship with your money. Food for thought!"

"I think it's important to be cognizant of your views on money," Mrs. Trevor added. "That includes how much wealth you want and why. And what you are prepared to do to accumulate wealth."

I agreed. "You need to decide if the journey which is often a struggle is worth the outcome. Everyone on their way to success has thought about giving up at least once. But what keeps you moving toward the final destination? The accomplishment? Your passion? Your drive?"

"I'm driven now to make some money," Sarah expressed, "and I'm passionate about going to school. I tell you if I ever had money, I would help whoever needed it."

Mrs. Trevor in her Goddess costuming observed Sarah carefully.

"I find the psychology of money interesting as a concept," I said. "My idea is to learn to master it or it will master you." I looked around the room, at each of the lovely women in their Egyptian finery. "Money! The desire to have money, acquiring it and worrying about it may be stressful driving forces in our lives. Money is energy, a symbol of exchange for our efforts. If we can determine its usefulness and how best to get it, then we can make peace with it. What are your views on money? How do you define it? How much money are you comfortable making, earning or acquiring?"

"The more money the better, right?" Nellie asked.

Mrs. Trevor paused then shared. "Money is the root of all evil! I remember hearing this when I was very young, around three or four years old."

"You, Mrs. Trevor?" Terri asked curiously. "I would never have thought that growing up with that kind of language and mindset you would still be able to accumulate as much wealth as you have."

Mrs. Trevor took a very long breath. "I was an orphan. My life changed once I left the orphanage. My sweet adoptive parents took me in when I was five years old. Growing up with them I realized that money does not need to be evil. The defining moment for that change in psychology was when my husband Gabby wanted to go into business. I thought that was a positive and productive approach to healing from our loss, so I agreed and supported him."

Everyone responded with awe and surprise.

"I believe in destiny," Mrs. Trevor continued. "You cannot change what is in store for you."

"I have learned the clearer you are about money and the more you define it, the better your chance of manifesting and acquiring it," Terri added.

Georgina took off her headpiece and gazed at it. "I remember a long time ago I desired more money to pay off all our debts, to be able to put the kids through school when the time came and to have a comfortable life style, nothing more. Later I learned that was tangible and achievable. But now everything has changed. I have to make new decisions."

I looked at Sarah and said: "You're excited to make money and I wanted to caution you."

She interrupted me quickly. "Yea, not to think that the more money I make the more I will get into debt, which is a negative mindset, right?"

I couldn't help but laugh. She grinned wildly and put both thumbs up.

Nellie had been quiet. She stood and walked towards one of the beautiful Pharaonic statues. With one hand she touched the turquoise veil hanging from the ceiling and with the other touched her giant Pharaonic red, cobalt and gold costume necklace and shared her story.

"I was born in a very rich family that treated me kindly and softly." She sniffled. "My family lost all their money during the war in the Middle East." She looked like a princess: beautiful, fragile and feminine with her gaze floating in the distance. "My father was a doctor but once he lost everything due to conspiracy he became an alcoholic and my mother grew rough and tough all the time. I had just graduated from nursing, which I resented even studying. I decided then that I never wanted to be like them or live anything similar to them."

She walked towards another statue, inhaled, touched the soft, flowy veils. The rest of us were silent, respectful, allowing her to continue.

"After the war I made a choice. I wanted something completely different because of what I had gotten used to growing up. I was very close to my aunt, my father's sister, who lived abroad. I was twenty one and asked if I could go and live with her. She agreed and despite my parents' opposition I moved in with her. Then I met Gerry, my husband.

We fell in love on our first date. He asked me to marry him within a year. He was already a multi-millionaire, a widow with twin girls. His wife had passed away during childbirth."

I was utterly amazed at how we had each had a totally different life, upbringing and aspirations, and yet we felt connected as women and as one human race.

Nellie continued. "I feel I bring a lot to the table and to my husband's success. Gerry was already a motivated, successful man, and I am a major force in supporting him. Gerry can focus on his work and I take care of everything else."

Georgina removed her Pharaonic jewelry and wrapped herself in one of the pink chiffon veils. Mrs. Trevor asked Sarah if she wanted to try her headpiece. Sarah's eyes filled with excitement. When she put it on, she started dancing around and singing. Terri joined Sarah, adding lyrics to the melody, and we all joined in.

When the song ended and everyone had settled into their seats again, I asked: "Did you know the Pharaohs in Egyptian times wanted to be buried with their wealth for a rich eternal afterlife?"

Sarah jolted back. "What?"

"Well, we are discussing different views on money and the psychology of money! I invite you to think deeply about these three questions. I know we addressed two of them before." I listed them, pausing between each.

1. If you had money, would you continue doing exactly what you are doing at your current job?
2. If you did not have the money you now have, would people still want to be around you and be your friend?
3. If you had a lot of money would you still work hard and sacrifice quality time with yourself, your family and friends?

"Interesting! Yes, I would continue my current work for now," Terri responded immediately.

Georgina offered the opposite point of view. "No, I'm not keen on where I work. I have important decisions to make."

Mrs. Trevor scratched her temple. " My son Jack works extremely hard to make sure our company grows to the next level. After my passing, Jack will become president of the company my husband Gabby and I built. Jack was a tremendous help when Gabby passed. He also helped build the company for the last twenty-five years. I hardly see him at family gatherings."

Nellie nodded. "I know what you mean, my husband Gerry also works all the time."

"I have one close female friend," Mrs. Trevor continued. "We have been friends for nearly seventy years. I love and trust her. But I know many people want to be around me because of my status."

"That's understandable," Terri interjected, "and not all of them will have genuine intentions."

"I believe one reason Jack works so hard is because he doesn't want to let me down, he wants to prove himself," Mrs. Trevor expressed with hesitation.

"I believe it's good to have money and wealth in order to enjoy life more and buy the things money can provide," I shared. "Many people equate success only with monetary success. My suggestion is to take a chance on betraying the thought of who you are! If wealth is for more than survival, if it is for creativity and exploration, it will be joyous. Is Jack curious and exploring the company for fulfillment or is he merely feeling responsible and pressured?"

"I wonder if he's trying to make sure you are pleased with the results, Mrs. Trevor," Nellie said.

Mrs. Trevor tapped her finger on the armrest and stared in the distance.

I winked at her. "I am sure Jack loves being part of the company. Success is not because you plan the success, but because you realize the success.

"Knowing you have a choice is important and making a choice equates to personal strength. Accept joy the way it comes. Pledge allegiance to whatever brings you the greatest joy.

"It is possible to turn fear into excitement and there are ways to get what you want fast. Every part of us as the animal we are is here to protect us, but we don't think of us as surviving. Adrenalin is released in order for us to survive. Adrenalin caused by fear is poison and we should get it out of our body as fast as we can. It affects our body and digestive system, our core temperature even changes. It affects our ability to think rationally because it's all about survival. There are many kinds of fear and we can personalize them or adjust to them.

"However, to be joyful is the task of life. When we are joyful or happy we are elated because we experience an endorphin field."

"I know we have talked about chaos, fear and joy to some extent. I can tell you that Jack loves the business," Mrs. Trevor commented, "but I can't say for sure about his motivations or passions. He has always been a private, quiet person and he certainly has changed over the years."

"Mrs. Trevor, I was merely curious about the characteristics, strength and aspirations of a man running a multi-million dollar company, whether Jack is following your footsteps or following his own purpose."

Mrs. Trevor nodded in understanding but without knowing the answer.

I continued. "Every idea and thing will die someday. We grieve when something dies because it is all consuming. The past is the act of dying. NOW is transition and a potential! When dreams die, nothing grieves them. New dreams come along! If you hold on to the past that has died, the soul thinks that's where you want creation to be so it can destroy it. From that chaos point, new creation can arise. Allow it. Chaos is always good because new is created. If you dwell on it, lament that it should not have happened, you bring it back to the present, as if you want it. If you still dwell on it after five days, there is something you want to continue. In five days, the animal thing has adjusted, knowing it has survived, but not the mental or emotional part of it. If you continue to grieve after five days, it is more of a personalized view. Realize and celebrate what you had, not what you lost or don't have. Keep valid filters."

Terri sat forward in her seat. "Are we still talking about Jack? I'm not sure I understand how this is relevant to him."

Everyone awaited my response.

"Well, if Jack fears losing the business or not being able to run the company successfully his emotions maybe triggered based on survival rather than exploration and curiosity as we have discussed. He can add his dreams to it and if there is chaos there will be an opportunity to create something new.

"The point is, if five days have passed and you survived the event, whatever it was, it was an emotional issue, not a physical or bodily issue. If you have a clear sense of self, you can control it by going through your filters. Do something about it; use the knowledge you have and learn to explore."

Nellie started walking around the statues again. "That's an interesting idea I can discuss with Gerry."

"Indeed," I agreed. "Embrace possibilities. Expectations and projections are illusion. By deliberately going outside of your normal, you break away from absolutes. Sometimes money issues are not just about survival. In this case, if I may, Jack might say he wants to make sure company profits are growing by at least fifteen or twenty percent every year to prove he is a capable leader. Then you may ask what is the essence that money gives Jack. Is it a sense of security, a sense of being loved or a sense of joy and pleasure?"

"I know we've talked about this, but I never thought about Jack this way," Mrs. Trevor said.

"I am not implying this is the case, Mrs. Trevor, but simply using it as an example. To prove you are a capable person by being creative could be a powerful inspiration; however, more joy comes from following your true passion and your dreams. Success requires responsibility, accountability and a truck load of passion and determination. Everything starts with a dream and a vision. Finances are no different."

Georgina unwrapped herself from the veil. "That makes sense."

Sarah was still taking notes.

I continued. "The idea is to monetize your true and strongest passion. I assume Jack is very comfortable financially. Would he still run the company if he didn't feel responsible? Is he truly passionate about it? In order to monetize, your purpose and intention must be very clear. Along your path, you can consciously and intentionally shift your way of thinking to believe in some thing or in some way. It is a conscious effort. You will notice a change of attitude when you start reprogramming your mind in a new way."

"I'm going to finish high school," Sarah confessed triumphantly. "Also, I have become really interested in law and legal matters."

We all applauded Sarah. The doorbell rang. The colorful, exotic food I had catered had arrived. We all sat like Goddesses, ate, laughed and celebrated being in one another's company.

After dessert I told them I was exploring the concept of applying the One Third Law to money as well! One third past, one third future and one third present.

"I'd be curious to know more about that," Terri said.

"Yes, and sometimes quantity has a quality of its own," I added. "Another aspect of the money relationship is to realize whether you earn your worth."

"How so?" Georgina asked.

I smiled. "The truth is we all want money, and we all want to be comfortable. But if you think about it, you will have a number in mind for how much you want to earn or how much you want to have. Let's say you earn $60,000 a year and wish to earn $100,000 a year, or you earn $300,000 a year and wish to earn over $1 million a year. The first question is, why are you thinking about the higher amount? And the second question is, what is holding you back from earning more?"

Georgina pulled her chair forward and leaned in.

"We have all heard: I can't get a raise; or it's not easy; or no jobs in my line of work pay enough. My definition of earning your worth is how much money you really believe you deserve to earn. If you think, well if I get x dollars a month I am OK or if I get a 2% raise a year I am good. My question is, why are you settling for that? Have you really thought about what your potential may be? You may feel that no one in your family has made a lot of money, whatever a lot may mean to you, or you aren't educated enough to make that kind of money."

"I'm with you!" Sarah exclaimed.

Georgina and Nellie agreed while Terri and Mrs. Trevor listened intently.

"Earlier I asked if you have any rules and ethics around money. Morals change, whereas ethics are yours to work with."

Everyone pondered.

"For example, every religion has the moral, do not kill. The moral is against killing, but if you kill another tribe, then you are a hero! Morals were the first survival tools and are mostly for self-preservation.

"My question, then, is making a huge amount of money morally repugnant? How about targeted giving, and giving generously when you don't agree with the ethics of how that money was generated and yet you agree with the morals?

"We as human begins are responsive and reactive. What we learn in life becomes our truth.

"In math two plus two equals four, which is a universal truth. That's what ethics create inside of us: a sense of identity where you never have to ask whether something is right or wrong. If you puzzle about an issue it's a moral issue. If you don't it's an ethical issue. I ask again, when you make decisions about making a very large sum of money, are they morally right to you or ethically right? Any questions or comments?"

I could almost see the questions percolating in their minds, but no one spoke.

"Morals are the force of society upon you, from the outside like a spiral. Ethics belong to you. Ethics are what you know is right from the inside. Ethical truth is your truth. So you can be ethical and impeccable but not moral and impeccable.

"In order to be ethical, sample the outside world for possibilities. Do the things you doubt you can do when morals have been forced upon you. Do something different to grow a sense of faith and a sense of ethics so that at the end of the day you are pleased to know you affected the world. You feel your effect when touched back by the world."

Terri explained that the same issue of morals and ethics existed in corporations as well. She was absolutely right.

"Another element," I said, "is the art of self-forgiveness. Often we lose our passion or drive along the way by focusing on our mistakes. We need to suspend the notion that we should have had the right answer, such as the right answer to invest properly or the right answer to make the right decision. One third belongs to you but the other two thirds is the Universe, which is against you being perfect. It's never all about you! It's OK if it doesn't go your way and it's also OK if you just don't get it. It's not about you. When you are uncomfortable, you can start doing something about it. It is your joy to do what is not your duty. To be enlightened is to know you do not fool yourself."

Sarah squinted in confusion. "Well if we're responsible for all our decisions and our lives then how does that count for one third?"

"Excellent question," I acknowledged: "According to the One Third Universe even though we are whole we are still only one third because of outside influences, forces and relationships. Even if we do everything in our power to get everything we want, it is still only one third.

"The idea is to impeccably know you! Because knowing you affects you and that affects the world in some way. The Universe sees you as joy and a spark. Your passion is your payment. With the right skills and knowledge, it grows to profit, and grows bigger and bigger."

"I love it!" Georgina exclaimed. "It's always passion that brings us joy, right? Like when my husband and I were in love and in passion I felt happiness and joy. What I'm hearing you say is that it's the same with everything including money matters."

"Yes, isn't that exciting?" I asked. "That's why it's imperative to always follow your heart and your dreams but first acknowledge and know your passion. Also realize that you never have the answers until you try, until you experiment."

"I am starting to see money differently!" Terri confessed. "I always had a strategic plan for myself and for my money."

"Terri, I am happy to hear you're looking at it with a different perspective now. Money is not real but the things it can do are real. When there is disharmony about money it relates to your sense of survival, whether real or not. If money is a matter of emotional survival then the brain goes myopic. Your self-identity becomes attached to it. One way to detach from disharmony is to turn it into fun and think, it is not you, it is just an idea of you. There is only universal truth, which is that effectively anything can occur, and it does not have to be exactly what you think it should be.

"To illustrate, let's say you think you have been attacked, but in reality you were not because if you were you would know. This trigger point is just a memory of collective consciousness; we react instantaneously without consciously being aware of it. As a human species we revert to our memory of archetypes and how we see them.

"For example, think of heroes. There are so many definitions, and each is an archetype of its own. Every unconscious memory you have is a distorted memory of the event. You keep fear there in the past as appropriate and draw on it if you need it. But for now, you say not here and not now. We think of these heroes and we compare ourselves.

"A useful purpose would be to recognize the power of it. Normally the first five days after being triggered there is no opportunity to recognize it as the body is still dealing with it. If there is adrenalin in the body, it affects the next thing and the next thing, and you associate everything with one thing which is to deal with the attack. After that initial period, we can increasingly deal with the situation in a useful way.

"The trigger point is instantaneous. You think, I am taking care of me. Five days later, you are still dealing with the effect of the event, which is not a physical threat and not about true survival. Understanding what you care about is the question."

Mrs. Trevor clarified. "So what you are saying is that when we experience fear that is not a physical threat we instantly go to the point of survival and instead we must emotionally detach from it and recognize that we are not threatened or in danger. However this emotional distress happens often when it comes to money?"

"Yes that is one way to describe it. Everything inside of you fear, anger, life experience serves a useful purpose if you let it and a harmful purpose if you blame it," I explained.

"When you know the difference between a real threat and a perceived threat, creativity results. As human beings we have the capacity to segment fear. To free up fear, adrenalin is released in small doses for preservation and large doses for escape. You can make fear small or large but pay attention to keeping fear as small as possible."

Nellie sat deep in thought, playing with her jewelry.

Georgina said: "I think I should pay attention to thoughts of how fearful I am when it comes to separating from my husband, when it comes to my children and how it will all work out."

Sarah and Terri offered her an encouraging smile.

"Exactly," I agreed, "but even if you take the example of fearing pain, you can do something different. Then fear stops being the manipulator and hurt goes away. Rather than amplify it, minimize it.

"Minimize what you think is actually threatened. Don't discount it as meaningless. Don't make it bigger than it needs to be. When you refrain from imagining it's larger, fear gets smaller.

"Or make the fear so large you can't conquer it. Once you do that, creative overwhelm results. Why? Because once you recognize it's not beneficial to fight it, you integrate it. You make it part of what is.

"When in fear, determine what's in danger. What is the real threat? Make it relevant. Then let your imagination exhaust fear. Deliberately amplify it. By going outside your normal pattern, you break away from absolutes. Take a chance on betraying the thought of who you are!" Play with life! When something pushes your buttons, do something different and do it deliberately to change the pattern. Of course you can change things! We always have choice.

"Provocative! Alluring choice of words," Terri commented.

"These are my words to explain the concepts. Feel free to use them differently," I responded. "The other part to this is that joy cancels fear. With deliberate joyous participation comes intentional effect, which is to start struggling and start participating. Make the fear relevant. All change is going to look like a struggle once you get used to it. To be as creative as quickly as possible, get to all the bright starry feelings, but don't fixate on self-protection.

"Look at the fear of what happens if you do something versus not doing it. When you are apparent about your life then you are apparent about yourself and it reveals your fear. Dance with fear: in time, in tune and in beat. The dance of fear equals passion (which is purpose), which is a point of discovery for how it serves you. Dance with the now even if you dwell in the past."

Terri poured herself a cup of tea. "I like the analogy. I think we all need to remember to use these tools when fearing whatever occupies our thoughts or emotions." She stretched out on the chaise lounge.

"I know many people obsess over money," I added.

Mrs. Trevor and Nellie perked up.

"One way to overcome that is to obsess deliberately. Don't let fear manipulate you. Instead of fearing money, deliberately decide you are going to obsess about it. That changes the energy and dynamics of it. If the obsession and fear are large enough to pay attention to, what is threatened that is not about you? Don't claim ownership, which is probably what you do. For example, let's say you obsess over unexpectedly losing a large sum of money in an investment, or are afraid of losing some of your assets for no valid reason. Consider what exactly is threatened here. Is it your ability to make wise decisions, your survival or your self-image?

"I can relate to this." Georgina leaned forward. "When I analyze my thoughts, obsessing over money is about not having my husband around. I can see it doesn't really make sense, mainly because I exaggerate not being able to survive without him."

"Yes," I acknowledged, "whether large or small, trust that you can cope with whatever it is. Make it the right size and know what is threatened. The key is to get to the anxiety, which is recognizing what is threatened. You break apart the fear; it may be a combination of a few fears, let's say six, and from that you get a different perspective, instead of one big fear that overwhelms."

"So true," Sarah said. "We just get into one big fear and freeze."

Nellie walked around the statues, playing with the veils and listening.

I continued: "What is the benefit of fear, you ask? How does fear add to your life? It has no effect, or you've got to get rid of those effects. Add passion without judgment. Don't think fear will destroy you. Start recognizing the fear, what it is. Don't laugh at it. Let the joy of your participation overwhelm the threat.

"Our fears are there to protect us. A turtle has its shell to protect itself and knows it. You decide what fears you will resort to for protection. You can encourage that protection, that hard shell for yourself. You pay attention to what is relevant. Relax enough to dance with fear. To do that, first you have to admit to your fear, that your fear is protection, an influential friend. The realm of fear is not so powerful! Only be afraid of what you choose to be afraid of and your life will be wonderful. Deliberately choose that."

"We never think about fear this way," Mrs. Trevor disclosed. "In my days I've faced many fears." She paused. "If I had these tools I would have faced them with less anxiety and less agony. It took me a long time to deal with them."

There was that look of regret again which I had surprisingly seen twice before.

Sarah took a veil and twirled towards Mrs. Trevor wrapping her in it. "My Majesty!"

It was so cute and funny, we all laughed.

"I love your sense of humor," Nellie complimented.

I was delighted to see the women reflecting on my words, making shifts in perspective possible.

"Take the fear now and make it excitement. Contemplate, recognize the benefit of fear. Fear's power keeps you from succeeding, so you won't fail. What does the fear serve? Ask! Then ask if it can be served differently. Find an event where you can deliberately press and have fear come to you. Find fear a form of excitement. Stimulate your fear but do it deliberately. Become sociopathic or narcissistic. Breathe in with your fear, benefit from it, and exhale fear's adrenaline. For example, breathe in protection, breathe out anger, anxiety, frustration. Notice when it appears. Where it appears.

"Convert disturbing adrenaline into exciting adrenalin. Over a period of years, all fears lose their protection. The farther you get, the more diverse fear becomes. When you feel fear today, it is an opportunity to explore and escape yesterday. Derive joy and excitement instead of fear and anxiety."

"The unending story of fear," Terri added.

"Someone of your status! How do you handle fear?" Georgina asked.

Terri sat up. " I focus on the task at hand. I don't think too much about fear. Exercise helps me a lot; it gets rid of excess adrenalin." She stood up while fixing her jewelry. " But this conversation has given me a lot to think about; some personal issues I wasn't ready to look at."

I thanked Terri for her honesty. "Identify the fears of yesterday and utilize them today. Explore the horizons of you! You understand that time heals everything or hoards everything. When did you learn this? Is it still valid? Go back to see when it was actually true.

"Start celebrating. Refocus on something different."

Sarah jumped with joy. "This is captivating. I think I'm really getting this and honestly I don't feel fear anymore: fear that I won't have money or that I will lose Anusha."

"I am thrilled Sarah," I smiled. "Escape fear and explore potential.

"Are fears in the category of effective truth? Take different sets of truths. Go to the most absurd, unbelievable end of it, and you'll see it's not true. Your fear is not true! For fears that control you, see the opposite. Don't be frozen by fear, just concerned; that's appropriate. If you fear something is not going to be successful, the opposite is that it's not supposed to be successful and you are doing it anyway.

"A sense of passion and a sense of participation without fear sends out ten dimensional vortices which then offers hope. It creates great enterprises. To increase joy, do things more deliberately. If you expect things to change quickly, you will not be happy. The problem is not that something is big, but that your view of it is big."

"So if I am joyful and passionate about being a lawyer that's good as long as I don't fear being a lawyer, thinking it's a big view of myself?" Sarah asked.

"Well, well, well, lawyer?" Georgina teased. "That would be awesome girl."

I felt inspired. "Fear is the impetus for celebration. Therefore, look at your fears joyfully. If you make a decision because of fear, it's probably the wrong decision or not the right decision. To convert fear to joy, you've got to be curious. There is an expectation of action; no action until it's taken. If it doesn't take place, it feels like counter purpose. Hope is the seed of passion. It's what you do with what you have. You can think, As long as I breathe, I can grow, discover, explore. Faith, on the other hand, does not require proof of participation. Everything is what it is. You explore because it is meaningful to you. By changing fear to happiness you look for the thing you've never seen; fear of the unknown."

"I understand all about fear of the unknown," Nellie said. "When I left my home country to live with my aunt I was passionate and hopeful. I couldn't speak the language and didn't have much, yet I charted into the unknown. Discovering a new life for myself brought a sense of joy and hope."

"The unknown does not have to strike fear in you as long as you have the strength to explore it," I responded. "What you don't know is not important to what you do know or can do along the journey and in the discovery. Don't fear the answers you have. The key is to embrace your inherent fears and know that it's a moment not a monument! Realize your impact on the world.

"Anxiety reveals opportunity when you turn fear into excitement. How to be bold without being told."

"Yes!" Mrs. Trevor agreed. "When we started our company, I was anxious as it was a matter of survival; as I saw it. But then there was a sense of hope and vitality to take the company further."

Terri told Mrs. Trevor she was brave.

"As we discussed," I said, "we can most likely achieve our goals and get what we want in life, even when there are challenges and setbacks, if we actively take steps and keep joy alive. Participation makes the journey more interesting. It is not the final outcome or destination that matters, but what we become in the process. There is great joy and satisfaction in knowing we worked toward our dreams and made them come to life. As humans, we value effort, so anything gained through our own efforts is appreciated. The journey makes us more successful and deeper individuals."

"Amen to that!" Georgina exclaimed.

"Although some may argue it would be great if a hero could just come along and make us successful or rich!" I continued. "Well, that thought could manifest based on our beliefs or expectations. Regardless, keep hope, reach for your dreams, and get what you want in life. You deserve to fulfill your potential and be happy. Don't let anyone tell you otherwise."

"Hmmm, I never thought of it that way." Nellie wandered around the statues.

"Each human being is given a life to spend and a life to observe with," I professed, "equal opportunity to create a want, to choose a motivator. With Creative projection, you can change fear to joy. But you also need to understand Detrimental Projection, which is that my view is the only view and it's my right to defend it.

"View yourself as; I have an effect; I can explore. The more I do, the more there is of me. And I must recognize when there is an opportunity to see things in a different way. One is not right and the other wrong; they're just different."

"So, it's all about creation?" Terri asked.

"Yes, and always create with passion, be it a delicious meal for your family or a rocket to travel to the moon." I agreed. "Every creation is to be treasured as far as Isness or Universe is concerned.

"Know you have a choice and making a choice is self-strength. You can control fear if you have a clear sense of self and look through your filters. Do something about fear; explore and use the knowledge you gain. Find confirmation that there is more than one view. Embrace possibilities and accept joy however it comes. Having allegiance to what you want brings you the greatest joy."

Georgina cleared her throat. "I am curious about the monetary issues of blended families while transitioning. You know my husband may move in with this other woman who may have children. How can we apply these teachings?"

"You caught me off guard, Georgina," I replied. "But on a practical level, yes you can certainly apply all that we've spoken about. First you need to take measures to make sure you are aware of your financial rights and obligations in terms of who is responsible for these children. Who is going to be the guardian and also be financially responsible for them? All of the children are the full responsibility of both parents unless the spouse who came in to the marriage with children does not have full custody of them."

"Well the reason I'm asking is because we are talking about how to handle fear when it comes to money and our relationships to ourselves and my mind just wandered off there."

"Actually, I am glad you asked. There is what is called a Relationship Entity. The best way to think of it is there is you, there is your husband and there is a third creature called the Relationship Entity. This Entity is affected by whatever interactions you have with one another. If you come from a place of need, and your husband doesn't, the Relationship Entity will spit out your need, which could cause frustration. If you both come from a place of need or want, it can work differently, however. In order for the relationship to expand you need to be out of self-protection and fear mode while being aware of your financial rights and obligations. If you approach your situation with fear and need, it can back fire. You are freer to create without self-defense."

Georgina nodded emphatically.

"There is also profit in relationships. If you supply one third you won't be profitable; if you supply two thirds you can't fail. If you put in more than what you take out, you are paying attention to what is yours. One third is half of what is possible. Universe wants to take you the most creative actions; it's not good if you hide from the Universe. Embrace yourself; do the thing that is yours and your potential increases. You'll know what is yours."

Georgina turned to everyone with a raised eyebrow. "You understand this?"

"Let me explain it the way I understand it," Terri said. "We need to be free of self-protection and fear in order to create whatever we want and expand. In addition there is another element which is the relationship we have with one another. If you are in fear about the transition with a blended family do your part without fear or need and with full knowing. If you can put out a little more you will increase the potential of what may be to your benefit."

Georgina thanked Terri while Mrs. Trevor poured tea for us all.

I asked if I could continue, and they all signaled yes.

"Your courage leaves a dent in the Universe. The key is to choose what part you want to defend, the relationship that is you, and act accordingly. In your case Georgina it may be a vulnerable thing to do but ask the following questions about yourself and your relationship with your husband especially when money issues arise. What do I want and need? Why am I in this relationship? What is missing from it to get what I want and need?

"The magic in relationships is changing your attitude toward them. The best way to leave a relationship is to join a relationship. Relationship Entities will spit out expectations because you feel disappointed if your expectations are not met. If the expectations are met three times, then it is an agreement, and a broken agreement causes chaos because there truly was no agreement. There is no recourse when those expectations are broken. The Relationship Entity, which is a breathing conscious being, spits out the non-needed thing so you can examine your expectation. It never hurts to ask; it almost always hurts to demand. To increase passion in relationships, refrain from being the decider."

Nellie asked if I could share an example of expectation in a relationship.

"Go up to an acquaintance, maybe at work or your gym, or some stranger you interact with and without prodding say: I really would love to take the time to listen to how things are going in your world today. I don't have the time for that now, but I do have the time to express that I care. Then watch what happens. You change one piece of the relationship and everything in the relationship changes."

They all burst out laughing.

"Find the grace of plenty." I paused. "Be happy in an unhappy world. Relationships are always on purpose. If you look at something that is positive and another that is negative, it is at cross purposes. Relationships are never at cross purposes; spitting out needs, rejecting needs, ignoring needs in favor of satisfying wants. If it feels unpleasant, someone put a need into the relationship. If you are paying attention and you feel comfortable, then it is yours to pay attention to. And if it is a distraction then that energy is part of it for a purpose.

"Your words, actions, choices and decisions affect the relationship you have with another. You may believe that if you disagree with someone else's opinion, that means they are wrong. Actually sometimes what you fail to see is that they may be coming from a totally different perspective. Let's say your boss is trying to do their job with minimum costs and effective results. They are as worried about or afraid of the situation as you are because they do not want to create conflict or chaos.

"And then some people are not considerate and don't care much about the consequence, they just want to be right or win the argument. In that case you decide if that's the type of person you want to work with or deal with. You can take control by not participating in the relationship despite the challenges.

"Procrastination is another cause of anxiety to be aware of when it comes to your relationship with money."

I offered some examples:

- I can't believe I can succeed at…
- I'm not sure what the benefit is. I'll wait until…
- I get an immediate benefit by not doing it versus…
- I believe I can be successful, but it takes too much work and I don't have the time.

"Observe how if you realize the nature of the attachment, it suddenly evaporates. Have you ever noticed that when you are faced with an emergency, you become a tower of strength and take care of your children, your partner, your family or parents? Something just takes over and you no longer think of yourself, you just dive in to the situation at hand. You pull it all together and do whatever is necessary. Where does this strength come from? Or the courage for that matter?

You can draw from this inherent quality. Although there may be times when the opposite happens, and you can't cope with emergencies.

"If you can put this kind of strength and courage towards your goals and dreams all the time, you will move mountains. By being aware you can make a conscious effort."

Sarah raised her hand. "We have talked about money and relationships, so I want to know about marriage versus common-law and cohabitation rights to avoid the usual pitfalls."

"Are you getting married or living common-law, Sarah?" Nellie asked, enchanted.

"I'm thinking about it. My girlfriend wants us to live together and be a family."

"It is quite common these days for a couple to live together instead of getting married," Terri said.

"Yes," I agreed, "and it's important to know there are differences between legally married and common-law relationships. The laws vary depending on where you live. Here, for example, same sex spouses in marriage or common-law situations are considered the same as opposite sex marriages or common-law partnerships. When you decide to marry someone, it is highly recommended that you come up with your net worth statement first.

"Considering our current law, although there is no right to property in common-law relationships, with some exceptions, there is a right to spousal support and child support. For example, Sarah, suppose you entered into a common-law relationship with Anusha, your two-year-old child from a previous relationship, and lived with your partner for ten years. Since you had full custody of your daughter when entering into the common-law relationship, and let's say you and your child were both supported by your common-law partner, if you were to end this relationship your partner would have to pay spousal and child support since she supported you and your child all those years."

"Well that's something to be aware of," Sarah said.

"Coming from a place of choice means you start walking the path of fulfillment, which is joyous," I continued. " By not making conscious choices chaos may result. The energy required to deal with the chaos depends on its specifics. The more chaos, the bigger the event. Notice, don't project; be an equal. What is yours and not another's? Don't protect, project or amplify. Make your decisions as personal as you can."

"Money, choices, relationships; a lot to think about," Georgina sighed.

"Money issues are not just about survival. For example, you might say: I would love to have a lot of money so that I could travel wherever I want to for as long as I want to. Then you may ask what is the essence that money gives you? Is it a sense of joy, a sense of security or perhaps a sense of pleasure? Once you find the essence of what you are looking for then it is much easier to follow it with joy. A person who is always worried about money is not truly wealthy."

It was getting late. I asked the group if they wanted to have dinner, but no one was hungry after nibbling all day. Everyone was happy with all we had covered that night. Each of them parted unwillingly with their Pharaonic headpieces and jewelry. We said good night and decided to reconvene soon.

Chapter 8

Your Wealth Creation

8

As much as we wanted to get together soon, we were not able to set a time when everyone was available. Maybe it was worth the wait as if the Divine had orchestrated magic. Terri informed us she had been telling a close acquaintance who owns a global company about us and our group. She told us he had invited us to have our next meeting on his private jet while he travelled to a client meeting for the day. We were ecstatic and after a few phone calls and texts back and forth we accepted.

The limo picked us all up and we arrived at the airport at eight in the morning. Terri introduced us to her acquaintance Chuck, a kind, sophisticated and distinguished man in his fifties. After we chatted for a few minutes he introduced us to the captain and first officer, who said we would be boarding in a few minutes.

We cheerfully boarded the breathtaking, luxurious, extraordinary jet. The dining section had twelve armchairs set up, the private meeting area could easily seat six, an open lounge area held leather couches, and on the second floor there was a beautifully decorated master bedroom. The two flight attendants greeted us and invited us to sit in the meeting area while Chuck sat elsewhere to prepare for his meeting.

I have always loved take-off and this one was exhilarating. I looked out at the sun above in the clear blue sky. The feeling was euphoric and peaceful at the same time.

I started our conversation. "Spirit or the Creator wants to create. Whether you love to joyfully cook gourmet dinners for your family or build sky scrapers, in the Universe's eye they are both creations. We need to honor the creation in each individual because where there is joy, there is life, excitement and fulfillment which propels us to expansion. By acknowledging creation, we become more alive as Spirit is appreciated and will generate more and deliver more creativity."

"Spoken like a true champion," Georgina said.

"We often value the creations that bring monetary gains," Terri added.

"Do you believe it's possible," I paused, "to have this much wealth?" I gestured to our surroundings.

Mrs. Trevor shook her head. "When we started the business I never thought I would ever own as much as I do but somewhere along the way I began to imagine the possibilities of having more and continued success."

"Right now, I cannot imagine owning so much wealth," Georgina whispered.

"Everyone wants to be rich and happy," Sarah jumped in, "but you know based on everything we have discussed not everyone would be able to achieve that."

"True," Mrs. Trevor said. "The minute details we need to look after, the important moments when we need to make essential decisions and the difficult times we go through which no one cares to talk about: the responsibility, the accountability and the journey! Not easy."

"Of course. Let your passion ignite you to action and greatness," I confirmed. "In any endeavor, the three elements we need to be cognizant of are our Energy, Time and Emotions. If we fail to manage any of these it's not going to be easy. For me especially, energy is crucial."

Terri straightened her shoulders. "I agree, and I need to exercise every day, otherwise my energy is not balanced and I cannot focus. It's like when you are in the zone or as you call it connected to the Divine everything flows smoothly."

"I still exercise three to four times a week," Mrs. Trevor offered with some pride.

"Wow, really? Kudos to you," Sarah enthused.

"Well, you know I do yoga five to six times a week and I asked my husband Gerry to join me. At first he was hesitant but then he tried a couple of times. To my surprise, he said not to tell anyone; he didn't want anyone to know."

"I am not surprised! I know some high rollers who think yoga is too weak, that it's for women."

Mrs. Trevor nodded in agreement.

"Energy management can be achieved through proper diet, exercise and good sleep. I continued. "Time management on the other hand is a different undertaking. You must have a proper plan with daily activities. One of the best techniques is to name the activity or task and attach a specific deadline with the date and time. We can attempt to meet every deadline but sometimes life wants its own way and the timing does not work out regardless of our plans. Tasks must be divided into categories and subcategories with the dates and times stamped.

"Regarding emotional management we need to acknowledge troubling feelings such as fear, sadness, anger, vulnerability or shame in order to make peace with them. We can ignore those feelings and focus on achieving our goals to build wealth or anything else for that matter, but emotional toxins will catch up with us. The important thing is not to give in and to continue working towards joyfulness.

"I have created an Alphabet Exercise. It's a fun, easy way to change our thoughts when we feel emotionally unsettled. Since words have power, you can change your neural pathways to focus on the desired feeling. Whenever you feel a certain emotion, name it and look at the first letter of the word that describes it. Then replace that word with a positive one that starts with the same letter.

"For example, let's say you feel melancholic, the word for the emotion starts with the letter M. Now use a positive word that starts with M, like magic, marvelous or magnetic. Once you replace melancholic with a positive word instead, you can say: I am magnetic, or I am marvelous. Use your Emotional Reserves, tap into a positive memory and feel a feeling that is magical or magnetic, to use the same example."

Georgina grinned. "That's a great exercise. I've got one I felt last week! Angry."

Nellie, Sarah and Terri all offered words: amazing, adventurous, awesome.

"Just like any other exercise it may take a bit of time to adjust to the new way of thinking or being," I added. "Now let's do another exercise: write down three desires you have, three fears you have and three accomplishments."

"Does it have to be about wealth?" Sarah asked.

"Not necessarily," I responded. "It can be one of your 3D's (Desire, Determination and Dedication), but we need three and since today's discussion is on wealth, you may choose it as one of your desires."

Mrs. Trevor stared out the window and Nellie checked out the furniture as she thought. After a few minutes Terri asked if she could share. We all paid attention as she communicated the following:

Desires

1. I desire to retire at the age of 50
2. I desire to have a net worth of ten million dollars at retirement
3. I desire to travel the world

Fears

1. I fear I will end up alone with no one to share my life with
2. I fear that I may not sustain my current income until retirement
3. I fear I will focus too much on work and miss out on life

Accomplishments

1. I was named one of the top ten CEO's in the country last year
2. I am the only female CEO who increased company profits by 35% in the country last year
3. I have a fit and healthy body

We all clapped at her achievements.

"Based on your past accomplishments and current desires do you believe you can fulfill those desires?" I asked. Terry paused briefly and responded yes. "Are you one hundred percent committed?" She said yes again. "Do you think your fears are so real that you have absolutely no control over them?"

"No," Terri confirmed. "I can manage especially since we have discussed a number of tools for how to handle fear."

"Can you see how by isolating and acknowledging your fears you can move ahead very quickly?" She nodded. "You can journal your realizations and declare your aha moments for reference."

"I like it," Terri added.

I continued: "Now one of the reasons I started with this exercise was to determine whether you desire wealth. My question is twofold: 1. How do you define wealth? And 2. What does wealth mean to you?

"In order to create wealth you must have the answers to these questions. You must be aware of your views and beliefs on wealth and money, know the exact dollar amount you desire to achieve it, the reasons you want the wealth, and what you are prepared to do to accumulate it."

"In the beginning," Mrs. Trevor said, "it can sometimes be hard to have an exact amount in mind, but in our case every year we reviewed the company profits and set a higher amount to strive for. And of course, at any given time you start with your individual Cash Flow (Budget) and Net Worth Statement. It's the same with a company, which is Profit & Loss (Income) Statement and Balance sheet. We always tracked both."

The flight attendant brought us refreshments, fruits and snacks. Chuck joined us and asked if we were enjoying the jet. We all said yes and thanked him for his generosity. Mrs. Trevor and Chuck began talking, and it turned out that Chuck knew Mrs. Trevor's son Jack. What a small world!

We were all jubilant and totally enjoying our private jet ride. Everyone agreed that Universe is mysterious! The more we feel gratitude, honor and appreciation the more doors open up.

After Chuck excused himself Sarah offered her appreciation: "I wanna thank you all for your friendship, support and guidance. You have had a profound effect on me!"

We all smiled in gratitude.

"Really, thank you all, too, I mean it," Georgina said.

"I'm in awe. My life has truly changed since we began getting together. I appreciate every one of you. And I would like to learn more ways for wealth creation," Nellie addressed me.

"Your husband is already quite wealthy, so why are you interested?" Georgina wondered.

Nellie shrugged with a twinkle in her eye.

"One way to create wealth is to invest a portion of your earnings," I explained. "The investment can become passive wealth."

I went on to outline various ways to generate funds:

1. You are employed, and you get a salary, or some sort of income. You can save or invest some of your income systematically.
2. You own your own business or businesses. You may be a sole-proprietor, in partnership or own a corporation. You may also own a franchise.
3. You may receive an inheritance.
4. You may receive a settlement from an insurance company, a court case or your ex-spouse.
5. You may have investment income.

Sarah looked puzzled, so I explained. "Investment income may be generated from different sources such as stocks, corporate or government bonds, guaranteed investments, mutual funds, ETF's, segregated funds, trust funds, cryptocurrency, foreign exchanges, mortgages where you lend money, or real estate. In real estate you may receive rental income, or buy and sell, or buy and hold, or buy, fix and flip. Or you might buy and sell businesses, including equity investing or venture capital. There are so many options available. You may choose to have a portfolio of investments like a real estate portfolio or a stock portfolio."

"Interesting," Sarah expressed.

"One important element to consider when buying or establishing a business is your exit strategy. Sometimes you may not wish to continue the business for a long time.

Terri shared that she had been diligently investing large sums of money over the last few years.

"That's excellent," I said. "The key to creating wealth is first to decide how much wealth you want to have in assets. Do you want to have the wealth in order to generate income for you, or you just want to have wealth in your name? The question is what do you want to do with the money? For example, do you want to have three million dollars to your name or are you thinking the three million dollars will provide income? Then ask yourself whether it would be all right if that reduces in value over time since you just wanted the income.

"I am always curious to know why people need a certain amount of wealth. What is it going to do for you?"

"I have become very interested in the subject," Nellie responded, "and have registered for a business course which includes accounting. I realize we start with a Cash Flow and Net Worth Statement as the primary criteria for success in any personal wealth building, or even a successful business."

Mrs. Trevor patted Nellie's hand. "I am proud of you, Nellie."

Nellie smiled with gratitude.

"A business must be profitable," I said. "A lot of attention must be given to expenses and costs because a business depends on the excess funds available to scale. Three key components are crucial in a business: 1. Profitability 2. Consistency and 3. Sustainability. This means the business must consistently bring in profit regardless of how the economy is doing.

"If you have a business or are thinking of owning a business, what is your vision for the company? Is it a local or a global company? How many people work there? What do you do there? How do you spend your time in the company? Do you have departments? Who runs those departments? Are you familiar with the different parts of the business? Who is your customer or client? How many clients would you need to make your business profitable? Where do you get your customers or clients?"

"Excellent questions," Mrs. Trevor said, " and it's important to have appropriate answers. I learned the hard way despite the fact that my husband Gabby was in charge of all that."

I agreed.

"Many years ago someone told me he had very little money saved and when I asked how much, he said $25,000. Another person told me he was thrilled he had accumulated a lot of money. I was curious to know how much, and he said $10,000. As you can see $10,000 is a lot of money to one person and $25,000 is very little to another. It's all relative, so it's extremely important to measure your goals and your finances against your own desires and what you would like to achieve."

"How much wealth should you have to be considered wealthy or affluent?" Terri asked.

"Some may look at your income and say you are wealthy, while others look at the amount of wealth you have accumulated," I answered. "On average half a million dollars a year income or a couple million dollars in assets will qualify you as a wealthy individual."

"I don't think there is a future for me where I work, especially now that I'm separated. I'll be going through with the divorce when the time comes," Georgina shared.

Sarah hugged Georgina. "Good decision!"

"I've actually started a program in early childhood education."

"I thought you were interested in decorating," Mrs. Trevor said.

"Yes I am, as a hobby, but I'd like to get my credentials in education, with an emphasis in autism."

"That's awesome!" Terri exclaimed. "Listen if you want extra money I can arrange decorating meetings with a few people I know. You might enjoy the work and make some extra cash."

"I appreciate that, Terri. Sure."

"That's a great idea; you can monetize your passion," Nellie suggested. "When you love what you do, you will make more money and have a better time doing your work."

I smiled. "Again, it's important to have purpose and intention for all you do. Your purpose may be to have joy and your intention may be to accumulate wealth. Therefore, taking steps will fulfill your intention and give you power. Your thoughts travel; breathe words into existence and see your intentions manifest into form.

"When you decide to own a business, you may choose to be a sole proprietor, in partnership or own a corporation.

"There are different types of corporate structure depending on the country.

A corporation continues to exist indefinitely unless terminated through a wind-up, amalgamation, or bankruptcy. This feature of continued existence is significant since there will be no deemed disposition of a business (other than the shares) on the death of a shareholder whereas a business carried on by a sole-proprietor or a partner will be deemed to have been disposed of immediately prior to the death of the proprietor or partner. This is another reason corporations are often used for estate planning purposes."

Mrs. Trevor adjusted her glasses. "We looked into all of this before my Gabby died. Corporations can be used for estate planning purposes for many reasons including continued corporate existence, succession planning and estate freezes."

"Exactly, Mrs. Trevor," I said. "In your case, I assume you didn't use a shareholders' agreement since you and your husband were the only shareholders."

"Correct, only because we trusted each other implicitly. But I would strongly recommend having that agreement regardless of who the shareholders are," Mrs. Trevor added.

I looked around the room to include everyone. "Such an agreement can set out the rights and obligations of the shareholders that go beyond the basic ownership of shares.

"Typically, a shareholders' agreement will provide for the orderly termination of the relationship between the shareholders if there is a future disagreement, death or disability of a key shareholder. Tax considerations play a major part in planning these agreements. The tax treatment of life insurance receipts, the availability of the lifetime capital gains exemption, the valuation of the shares, and many other issues must be considered."

"Yes it's crucial to look into all of these if you have a company or corporation," Mrs. Trevor said.

"Tell me more about mindset when it comes to wealth," Sarah asked.

"It's necessary to keep a positive mind set when it comes to money; however, to overcome a negative mindset, you may ask yourself what is the main thought preoccupying you? Notice what else is attached to that thought.

"For example, you might have a dialogue in your head: I don't know if I have enough money to pay my rent or mortgage. Well, I should have it! I make enough money. But what if I can't make it? I should be able to make it. I don't care about money anyway. I really don't want to work. If I had a richer partner or a better partner I wouldn't have to work. I am stupid for not being with someone more successful; but I love him or her... And on and on it goes.

"Do you see the trap? How that just takes space in your mind?"

"Someone with a lot of wealth can still go through the same process of negative dialogue," Terri acknowledged.

"Yes, and if the negative dialogue is constant, it's exhausting and may not turn out well," I continued.

"One way to avoid such a dialogue is to first state the goals short-term, medium-term, and long-term that are important to you. Then every time your negative thoughts are overwhelmingly obsessive go through the following process in order to stop the dialogue."

I offered: "Check your own mental dialogue:

- Assessing your thoughts, implement a programming technique using the Growth Mindset discussed earlier. Ask yourself how someone with a Growth Mindset would handle this.
- Do a Net Worth Statement and Income & Expense analysis. Find out how far you are from your targeted goal. Take steps towards fulfilling your desired outcome.
- Appreciate where you are in the journey. Give gratitude.
- If you are still feeling bombarded by negative thoughts, use the Cognitive A, B, C technique."

Nellie's eyes glittered with joy.

"If you are unsatisfied with your work," I said by way of example, "look for a new business or position. Decide what you love to do, use

248

the same reprogramming techniques mentioned. Take an inventory of where you are in your career, how many more years you will be working, how well off you are financially. Check to see whether you can turn your love into a business and whether you can make the business work."

"That makes sense," Sarah said.

"If you are not happy in your salaried position, take inspired action and look for other opportunities. Change companies or take another position in the same company. You may need to upgrade your skills. Refer to what brings you joy and take steps towards your desires," I advised.

"Sometimes in business our personalities clash," Terri said. "Have you ever been in a situation where you are quite nice and try very hard, but the other person is mean, impolite, angry or controlling? It might be a good idea to step back and look at the situation or the person and say, well that's not my issue."

"We cannot change anyone unless they want to change, and it's not our responsibility to be a savior," Mrs. Trevor warned us. "One point of caution is if your buttons are pushed no matter how nice you are, and feel annoyed by the other person's behavior, it might be an issue within you that needs to be addressed. This can often happen in the workplace. You do have a choice as to how you respond."

"Yes," Terri agreed. "Let's take a step back and look at a hypothetical situation concerning an employee and a boss at work. Ask yourself:

"1. Am I really happy in my position, even if my boss were a different person?
"2. Was I looking forward to working with the boss when I was interviewed for the position?

"If the situation is unreasonable, as an employee you can go to your boss and say whatever you think you should say or even quit. Just as an additional point, your boss probably has issues and fears of their own not that you necessarily need to know about them but just know they've got their own problems."

"Controlling every single outcome is taxing," I responded. "To keep your passion alive regardless of type of work try different things including surprising yourself with new ideas, novelty and new experiences. Reminisce about past successes and be attentive."

"If you are entrepreneurial and want to start your own business you must be a leader who leads with conviction, passion, purpose and a vision. A leader is not afraid to chart the way and has the courage to go first."

"In order to succeed in business you must establish solid relationships. There must be synergy or chemistry with your clients, and they must like and trust you. You must be transparent, add value and be respectful," Mrs. Trevor added.

Terri agreed.

"Absolutely," I voiced. "It takes more than desire to run a successful business. Many skills are necessary because accumulating enormous wealth depends on managing the business successfully."

"Wealth creation requires communication and people skills, since most often wealth is created through interactions with others. If you don't have people to support you and implement your vision, it will be a long and time-consuming process."

The flight attendants came in to clear the table and asked if we would like anything else. We thanked them and said no.

"Do you know there is a perception we're encouraged to believe that females do the task the right way while males to excel at it?" I asked.

"Love that concept!" Georgina chuckled.

"We discussed the Relationship Entity, which is a conscious, breathing creature. In any relationship including business relationships if you are uncomfortable ask yourself why you care. Why do you think what you think is true?"

"I understand that in a personal relationship but why is it necessary for a business relationship?" Sarah asked.

"Excellent question." I took a breath. "Building a large amount of wealth almost always requires trustworthy, working relationships. These may include your team, your employees, or simply your clients.

"If you are not at ease in a relationship, ask yourself what is my need that needs to be satisfied. If you're coming from a place of need, the Relationship Entity will spit it out and cause an upset in the relationship. Relationships satisfy wants. This is why coming from a place of passion and excitement fuels the relationship."

"I remember we talked about this in my personal relationship with my husband," Georgina said with excitement.

"Correct," I said. "If both parties come from a place of need, it can work. For example, let's say you have a manufacturing company, and you need a buyer overseas. If that buyer is desperately looking for your specific product, then the business deal will go more smoothly. But if the buyer has many options and does not need your company, you may be upset if that particular buyer is the only one available. Any relationship is more joyous when coming from a place of want."

"If you resent a situation, something or someone you always end up leaving in the end," Mrs. Trevor said wisely, "or end up getting sick if you stay." She looked through the jet window.

"For sure," Nellie confirmed.

"Add currency to your emotional bank," I added. "It's a good investment!" I winked.

"To build and sustain wealth you may be participating in a big community; be it at work or in a group. You may be involved in different relationships and it's a good idea to assess the nature of each. The difference between obsession and expectation is a sense of deliberation. Be clear on the purpose and intention of the relationship so it attracts more energy to the relationship. Let the relationship itself excite passion. Trust the relationships. Stay on purpose."

"I find this information quite useful as I intend to be involved in my husband's company," Nellie offered.

I smiled. "Relationship Entities don't just fulfill wants, needs and desires; they also fulfill what we don't want, need or desire. Relationship Entities are neutral and purposeful.

"Once we are clear about the nature of our relationships in terms of our needs, wants and desires with others, we can easily remove the parts that don't work and participate joyously."

"I don't think about my work relationships like this, although I can see the benefit," Terri said.

"I understand," I responded. "It's why employee and employer relationships are often distant. If we are more conscious of our relationships then there will be more joy.

"I particularly support relationships where there is growth, joy and expansion. Relationships are the life blood of self-awareness. The difference between boredom and joy is that joy leads to new feelings. If you lose the positive and negative power of surprise in a relationship, you will get more surprises. The best way to deal with an issue is to have your back to each other by not blaming one another and let the relationship take over.

If you let relationships do what they naturally do, you'll have an easier time. It never hurts to try."

I saw emphatic nods.

The captain announced we would be landing in twenty minutes, just enough time for me to make my final and most important point.

"The key to wealth is wealth consciousness," I said. "A person who is always worried about money is not truly wealthy. Studies have shown that wealthy people make charitable donations. As much as automatic savings and investing are a must in accumulating wealth, automatic donations are also an important element. Remember this fundamental principle of the Universe: when you give without worry or feeling a lack of money, you will attract more money. Give with love and joy, and you will receive multifold.

"Heart-based decisions are more satisfying than decisions from your mind. In decision making if you can connect your mind and your heart you will make wise decisions. Tap into your Inner Wisdom to make wise decisions in your business and your life."

"Well said." Mrs. Trevor clapped.

"Focus is a powerful tool to take us further in life. To create wealth, make a choice backed by inspiration, passion and laser sharp focus. Define exactly what it is you want and have a clear idea how to go about it. Have faith and trust and proceed with the expectation that you will succeed. You never know the outcome until you try."

We had arrived at our destination. Chuck invited us to have lunch at his client's winery while they met. We agreed joyfully. Lunch was magnificent, on a private patio looking at acres of grape vines, soaking in the sun and savoring a delicious meal paired with wine.

We had a wonderful afternoon and headed back home on the jet.

Chapter 9

Your Legacy

9

nother few weeks passed. Nellie sent us an invitation to meet in one of the city's most upscale, unique art galleries. She said her art work had been showcased there some time ago along with known international artists and sculptors. We thought it was a great idea to visit the gallery and see interesting art. We all arrived at the same time and were greeted by a middle-aged couple who owned the gallery. An animated Nellie introduced us. The woman appeared cultured, wearing an artistic, elegant flowy maxi dress with simple but expensive gold and silver jewelry while her husband stood dignified and refined beside her in a bow tie. The couple looked stunning together. They welcomed us to their gorgeous place. We spent about an hour looking at the rare and exclusive paintings. The sculptures were astonishing, heart-stopping in their size and diversity. The gallery lighting was perfect, projecting shadows on bare walls to lend a mysterious, enchanting feel.

Nellie told us the owners were friends of her and Gerry and they knew we needed a private place for our meeting. We were escorted to a private lounge with unusual armchairs and chaise lounges, posh area rugs, exceptional art work, vibrant paintings and sculptures that looked alive and breathing. It was truly a majestic feeling to be in such a room. On the table were mouth-watering appetizers, fruits and a variety of beverages.

"What a place!" Terri burst out jubilantly.

"I've never seen such exquisite art," Mrs. Trevor admitted.

We admired our surrounding in the private lounge and chatted with the owners for a little while. Then they excused themselves and left us in our glory.

"For the longest time we have been talking about creating our desired life. When you live you create and when you leave this world, you leave your creation behind. What would you like to leave behind?" I asked.

Everyone was glowing with inner light and a peaceful aura.

"I'll go first since I am the eldest here," Mrs. Trevor said with a smile. "I'll leave a large sum of money behind." She laughed. "I am not an Egyptian Pharaoh so I can't take it with me!"

It was odd, I had never seen Mrs. Trevor so joyful or open.

Nellie was almost shaking with barely contained joy. "I am pregnant with a baby boy!" Tears of joy rolled down her cheeks.

She had been waiting for this child for an exceedingly long time. We were almost breathless with joy for her. Mrs. Trevor walked over to give her a big hug, as did we all while congratulating her.

"Life is amazing. I love life! I love surprises!" I claimed.

"Absolutely," said Sarah: "I have news of my own."

"Bring it on," I encouraged.

"I graduated from high school and will soon be going to university to become a lawyer."

"That is wonderful news!" Georgina hugged Sarah while the rest of us raised our glasses to her.

"I am truly proud of you Sarah. You've done a wonderful job!" Mrs. Trevor enthused.

Sarah put a hand on her chest. "In gratitude, thank you."

I felt so exhilarated, I couldn't sit still. It felt as if I was in a different era, a different time zone; being in that environment was surreal.

"There are so many beautiful art pieces here. How did the owners acquire them all? They must have spent a fortune!" I said.

"Marianna's grandfather was an art dealer. He loved to collect antiques. Then he passed the business on to his son, Marianna's father, and he passed it on to her," Nellie explained. "She inherited everything as an only child. She has loved art since she was young and helped her father manage the business. Her work is one of a kind."

"Does Marianna have any children?" Georgina asked.

Nellie shook her head.

Sarah cracked me up when she said: "How about that success plan? Isn't that what it's called?"

I laughed. "Succession plan, especially for business owners. Do you know a high percentage of new businesses do not last more than five years? Very few businesses last more than ten years and only a few lucky ones last a lifetime. Let's say you have worked hard to build a multi-million dollar company, like Mrs. Trevor. Or your parents started the business and you perhaps helped them grow it. What will happen when you're gone but you want the business to continue?"

"Very good question," Sarah pondered. "I guess this might be your friend Marianna's case?" she asked looking at Nellie.

Mrs. Trevor shifted in her chair and sat up straight. "Succession planning is absolutely necessary. Do you know how many times I have seen businesses fall apart after the owner has passed away?"

Terri agreed. "Yes, of course. Sometimes the children are not interested in the business. What do you do then?"

Mrs. Trevor shared what she had done. "As you know, my son Jack has been our right-hand man and contributed significantly to the growth of our business. My second son Patrick has worked in the business part-time on and off helping out when needed, and one of my daughters Nathalie works in the company full-time. My other two children never got involved in the business because they had no interest.

"Jack will take over the company as majority shareholder and become the president upon my passing. I have considered my two other children who have worked in the company. But the reality is my estate is partially the company and partially my own assets."

She took a long pause. We watched her face in anticipation of what she would share next.

"In addition, what I have not shared with you before is that my daughter Sonia died of cancer at the age of forty-two." Our jaws dropped, but she raised a hand signaling us to wait for her to finish. "She left three children who will receive part of my estate along with my other grandchildren."

We all expressed our condolences on Sonia's death, but Mrs. Trevor kept reverting back to the succession conversation.

"Now there are a few issues; one; dividing the estate assets appropriately, two; taxes payable which will be enormous both on company growth and my personal assets as some have been tax sheltered for a long time but will become taxable upon my passing, and last but not least my son Sebastian is single, and he will inherit a sizeable sum. He is in his late forties and if he decides to get married and share the inheritance with his wife I cannot directly decide what should happen to the money unless I establish a trust which could cause resentment."

"So, it's true the more money you have, the more problems you have." Sarah rolled her eyes.

"It's better than not having it!" Terri retorted.

Georgina grumbled: "But you know average people don't have these kind of issues."

"Sometimes," I said, "the exact amount of funds in the estate is not as important as the concerns you may have over who gets what and how much. For example, Mrs. Trevor has five children. One question would be since Sonia has passed on, do her children get Sonia's share of the estate in addition to whatever their own shares may be? If the answer is yes then let's divide the entire estate into six for a moment, not considering the grandchildren. Now Jack has worked really hard to grow the company, will he get a bigger share? That is a decision Mrs. Trevor may have considered. In this case equal distribution means that each of Mrs. Trevor's children who are the beneficiaries will get one sixth of the estate whereas fair distribution might be that her oldest son Jack will get a bigger portion since he was instrumental in building the family business."

"Very interesting." Terri leaned forward.

I continued: "These questions and issues may be concerning and must be dealt with. Your decision as to how to distribute your assets will be crucial in order to put strategies in place to ensure your wishes are fulfilled in the most tax efficient way. If the business must stay in the family, provisions have to be made to make sure that family members run it once you are gone. There are many different strategies available and each scenario must be considered carefully before choosing a solution."

Mrs. Trevor walked towards a beautiful painting hanging from a thirty-foot ceiling and stood next to it. "Well, there are additional issues to think about. Jack is in his sixties and he needs to groom a successor. One of his children is half interested in the business, we'll see what happens. My other daughter Elena is divorced with four children. Her oldest daughter is quite keen on the business, but Jack and Elena don't get along too well, and this causes tension."

"My, my!" expressed Nellie.

"There is that inheritance risk of who gets what," I agreed. "That's why it's really important to have an updated will. Sometimes people think it's easy: I know how much money I want to give to the people I care about. Or they might say, I don't really have anything to give. All sorts of assets are passed on as inheritance. They may be investment assets or personal assets such as your jewelry, furniture, car or boat, or certain collections like antiques, cars, music and much more. The question is, how do you divide up your estate? Why do you divide it up that way? Do you favor one child over another? Are you going to leave one of your children out of your estate because you disapprove of their choices or lifestyle? Each family has its own dynamics." I looked around the room. "We are emotional creatures. Not everything is numbers," I added.

Mrs. Trevor had taken her seat again. "Elena wants the house as part of her inheritance. A lot is at stake because there are so many beneficiaries, including my fourteen grandchildren and the charities I intend to leave sizeable gifts to."

"That's very generous," Sarah commented.

Mrs. Trevor continued. "One of my grandchildren, Elena's daughter, is hooked on drugs." Sarah looked at Mrs. Trevor in disbelief. "She is always rude to me, impulsive, impolite, and always causing trouble. I'm terribly upset with her. I wanted to teach her a lesson. I cut her out of my will. In any case her mother Elena will have enough that she'll leave her daughter an adequate amount; more than she deserves." She paused. "I'll give more to Jack. It may not be equal but it's definitely fair."

"Yes, it is a bit complicated," I said. "Some people may even contest the will. Certain items may have sentimental value and that could trigger a fight between siblings. Other times depending on the type of business structure, things can go wrong and end up in the hands of the wrong beneficiaries, especially when you own a business."

Sarah asked if I could quickly go over the types of business structure. She said it might help if she chose corporate law.

I nodded. "A sole proprietorship is a business structure where an individual personally conducts business and the individual's profit and losses go directly to the individual's income tax return.

"A partnership is where two or more individuals carry on business together on an ongoing basis and share the profits and risks of the undertaking. If the partnership is without a partnership agreement, net profits are shared equally.

"A business owner might choose to operate the business as a corporation rather than a sole proprietorship or a partnership for a variety of reasons. One of the primary benefits of incorporation is Limited Liability of the shareholders for the risks of business operations. Risk is limited to the capital invested in the corporation. However, many creditors of a private corporation will require the shareholder to personally guarantee its loans to the company. A corporation is a separate legal entity distinct from its shareholders. One advantage of a corporation is that the corporation can continue its existence even when the shareholder(s) pass on. The techniques and strategies to put in place in order for your business to continue after death will vary depending on the structure of your business."

"The success or failure of any business," Mrs. Trevor interjected, "depends on the company profits, the dynamics of the relationship between the business owners and the longevity and sustainability of the business among other factors. In order to leave a legacy, owning a corporation is one great way."

Terri served us appetizers while Sarah poured some beverages. Georgina admired an abstract painting and asked about Nellie's art and previous exhibitions.

After a few minutes of indulgence I called us back together. "The joy and peril of giving. A lot of people love to give: their time, their energy, their money. Giving brings a sense of joy and a sense of community. Sometimes people cannot say no and just keep giving to whomever asks."

"Yah, tell me about it," Georgina groaned.

"I like to distinguish between giving voluntarily and out of joy versus giving out of obligation or lack of control. Some give due to their religious or spiritual beliefs like tithing say ten percent and some give to get tax credits. When you are willing to give your hard earned money because you feel you are helping, to build a school or a hospital or whatever it may be, and at the same time you receive tax credits in order to pay less taxes, you are benefitting both emotionally and financially and even perhaps spiritually," I added.

"However, sometimes you want to give financial assistance to someone close to you, a friend, a sibling or a family member to help them out. Now if this is a temporary situation it's OK but sometimes they keep coming back again and again asking for your help. This is when things become stressful and you continue giving without a tax break or feeling satisfaction, because now you have enabled another person to rely on you without any positive results."

"I was that person who couldn't say no," Georgina shared. "Ever since I can remember, I kept giving and giving. Even when I loaned money, I couldn't get it all back. On the other hand my sister Alia wouldn't share a dime. Now she is a top-notch actress who doesn't give a hoot about anything. She makes tons of money probably millions. She tries so hard to accomplish more: more money, more popularity, more fame. She is gorgeous and very selfish."

"You have a rich sister?" Sarah asked.

Georgina just huffed and rolled her eyes.

Mrs. Trevor said she had always loved tithing and giving charitable gifts.

"Charitable gifts can be given during your life time or after death," I continued. "You may give cash instead of certain assets, such as stocks or mutual funds or even life insurance proceeds."

Mrs. Trevor made a pyramid with her hands. "Oh I am glad you mentioned that. I wasn't sure. I am in the process of revising my will." She paused. "And I will include all my grandchildren." She inhaled deeply. "Another great way to leave a legacy is memorable charitable giving."

The owners came in to check on us. We were delighted and complimented them on their gallery. They told us lunch would be served in half an hour.

Terri was glowing with a twinkle in her eyes. Nellie asked if she was happy about anything particular.

"I met a nice man," Terri admitted. "I'm quite enraptured."

Mrs. Trevor asked her to tell us more.

"Well, he is 6'2" with gorgeous hazel eyes and dark hair, an incredibly handsome man. He has never been married and is forty-five years old, which is seven years older than me. He is kind and loving. He is different than the type of men I usually date."

We all smiled and told Terri how happy we were for her.

Nellie asked: "What type of men do you usually date, if you don't mind me asking?"

"Not at all," Terri replied. "Usually business men and entrepreneurs. But this one… I don't know," she sang.

"If he is a good man, make sure you keep him," Mrs. Trevor said.

"Well it's a fairly new relationship, but I have a good feeling about him. He is very attentive; he works but is not too interested in building a lot of wealth. He is OK financially, not too driven in that department." She chuckled.

We all wished her well in her relationship.

"When one door closes another one opens!" Georgina exclaimed. "I have done a lot of reflecting, thinking and soul searching and have decided that I will go through with the divorce without contemplating a reunion."

Sarah asked: "Isn't the proverb for your own life?"

Georgina just shrugged.

Nellie spoke softly and compassionately. "Georgina, if you think and you know that is the best decision for you, then it is."

Mrs. Trevor confirmed with an encouraging nod.

"I have a confession to make," Terri said. "In the beginning I was envious of you and your relationship with your husband. You were so happy talking about the love you shared. I have never shared deep love with anyone. Hopefully soon. It's ironic that you are leaving your relationship and I'm joining one." She put her hand on Georgina's. "I am really sorry about being envious."

Georgina smiled sadly and a tear dropped onto her cheek. "I need to thank all of you for your support and friendship as I couldn't have done it without you. I will finalize my divorce as soon as possible, focus on my childhood education studies and get my credentials so I can work in the field. My son Eric is highly intelligent but has a hard time expressing. I'd like to be able to do something for autistic children. Frankly that should be my legacy."

"Wow, that was profound." I hugged Georgina and gave her a kiss.

266

"That was a big decision! I am sure it wasn't easy." Mrs. Trevor comforted her.

Georgina nodded in silence while looking at the floor.

"Legacy has a joyful ring to it," I said. "As we go through life, we gather knowledge, wisdom and experience. We create, enjoy life and leave a mark. The interactions we have with one another have a profound effect on each of us. Legacy need not always be a life-changing world event.

"However, most often we associate legacy with leaving a large amount of wealth. One area I find interesting is Intergenerational Wealth Transfer, where wealth passes from one generation to another and can also skip one generation.

"The psychology of money is different in different age groups therefore the impact money and wealth have on each generation is different."

I listed the approximate birth dates of each generation:

- Greatest Generation: 1910-1924
- Silent Generation: 1925-1945
- Baby Boomers: 1946-1964
- Baby Bust or Gen X: 1965-1980
- Millennial or Gen Y: 1981- 1997
- Millennial or Gen Z or I: 1998 -2012

"For example, the Silent Generation focused on wealth accumulation whereas Baby Boomers think of themselves as entrepreneurs, enjoying their life style and interested in hobbies. The Baby Bust or Generation X are technology savvy. Millennials or Generation Y seem to be more environmentally conscious.

"Although most of our belief systems and value systems stem from our upbringing and family environment, it appears that each generation has a lot in common due to age, the actual culture of the generation and their general social and economic environments. Therefore, it's crucial to look into all these aspects simply because their thought processes and expectations are different, including their method of communication (like sending a post card versus an e-card, texting versus e-mail)."

"I see it first hand in my family," Mrs. Trevor shared. "The generation gap between myself, my children, grandchildren and great grandchildren. It's certainly an experience. Since we are on the topic of legacy I'd like to share something that has been close to my heart. As you know I really wanted to be a ballerina, but I didn't think I could ever pursue that dream. My desire was so strong that I practically forced Sonia to go to dance school, but my daughter never followed through. She just didn't have the discipline required. Sonia actually wanted to be a lawyer, but she ended up in a serious but non-fatal car accident in her second year of university. As a result she never continued her studies."

Mrs. Trevor cried in pain as we sat silently and sent her our love.

"Sonia had her whole life ahead of her." She inhaled deeply and exhaled slowly. "After a few years of intensive physical therapy, she got better. She married her high school sweetheart and gave birth to three beautiful children. A few years later cancer got the best of her and Sonia died."

I watched everyone's reactions. There were tears and I felt the grief that filled in the air.

"I was ravaged," Mrs. Trevor continued. "I cried and cried, mourning the loss of both my children but nothing changed. Losing two children?" Tears rolled down her face. "I made the funeral arrangements with my son Jack. Her husband couldn't deal with Sonia's death."

Mrs. Trevor stared at a painting across from her.

"Sonia's daughter is a talented musician. She plays the cello and gives concerts internationally. She is the closest I ever got to art."

"Life…" Georgina sighed.

Mrs. Trevor's face relaxed into its sweet, innocent composure. "Life makes you humble! I learned wisdom through time, hardship and disappointments. I would argue with Sonia when she didn't want to go to dance class. She didn't care for it and I was forcing my heart's burning desire and passion onto her so I could live vicariously through her."

She inhaled to the count of three and exhaled to six, the calming breath ratio of 1:2, I had taught them. We all joined in.

"The death of a dream!" she continued. "Over time I learned that to be sweet, loving and understanding is the way of life. And recently as we have been talking, I've been able to forgive myself. For the longest time I thought that if I didn't push her so hard maybe she wouldn't have had that accident and maybe she wouldn't have gotten ill. And maybe, and maybe… But life is what it is, and we accept, and we forgive."

Sarah wiped her eyes and pulled herself together. "Thank you so much for sharing, Mrs. Trevor."

We all looked at Mrs. Trevor's teary face then gazed into space, projecting love and understanding.

A few minutes later, with perfect timing, the owners came in and invited us to join them for lunch. Lunch was set up buffet style on a few luscious round tables of varying sizes and heights in between a few fountains. It was a heavenly array of colorful, delicate tapas. The dishes were artistically presented and exquisitely tasty. The hostess gracefully served each of us a delicacy, and asked Nellie when she could expect her paintings in the gallery again.

Nellie beamed and shrugged.

"I could definitely get used to this!" Georgina said.

We all agreed while consuming the delicious lunch with a huge appetite.

After lunch we walked around the gallery a little more to admire the art. One particular sculpture had gotten my attention. Nellie explained some of the paintings to us. We listened, we talked, and we enjoyed our experience. The owners had to attend to some clients who had just arrived but welcomed us to stay as long as we wanted. We went back to our private lounge to continue our discussion.

"As human beings we want to make a mark and know that we have an effect," I began, "that our creation is unique and that we matter! Our existence and our creation bring joy to the Universe. My question to you is how would you like to be remembered once you leave this planet?"
Sparkling silence filled the air.

"My wealth and my family are the creation and legacy that I will leave behind," Mrs. Trevor replied.

"Of course, family is very important" Nellie said, massaging her belly with both hands, "and I suppose my art and my kindness if I may say so, will be my endowment."

"I assume what we leave behind must be measurable, attainable or tangible, right?" Terri asked.

"My definition of legacy goes beyond the physical. It may be an impact, a change in tradition or culture, a change in the political arena, or merely a new innovation or common positive change left for humanity," I explained.

"Yes, I like that," Nellie said. "I believe in kindness but how would one consider that a legacy?"

"Your kindness has an effect and warms people's hearts; it encourages them to love. Perhaps they will remember you that way," Georgina remarked.

"Spoken like a true philosopher." Terri smiled and Mrs. Trevor clapped.

"That is a profound statement," I said. "Our creation belongs to us, but we do affect everyone, be it in small or big ways. When we create out of passion and love, we get to benefit from the results of that creation and experience the joy. And if that affects many then we are remembered for it."

"How?" Sarah asked.

I leaned forward. "For example, if you love to dance and you perform on different stages or platforms you affect many who watch your performances; then you are remembered as a great dancer. I call this your legacy. Another person may build a castle or a hospital and that would be their legacy." I added. Everyone was captivated. "I always think, if tomorrow was my last day on earth have I done everything I wanted to in life, and did I have joy? And I wonder how I would be remembered."

Terri nodded and played with her hair. "Then the way you define it, legacy is not just financial wealth, it's the impact and the profound effect you leave behind, correct?"

I smiled and said yes.

A grin flickered on Sarah's face, but her eyes said her thoughts were a bit far away.

A feeling of camaraderie and mutual appreciation passed between our glances.

At that moment I felt a strong unbreakable bond between us that had touched my life with joy, compassion and gratitude.

Mrs. Trevor sat straight, looked at each of us with love. She made a pyramid with her hands as she often did. "Indeed it has been a pleasure knowing you all. My birthday is a month away. It is with joy that I invite all of you and your families to join me to celebrate my 85th birthday."

We were ecstatic and Sarah cheered.

"I have arranged a big celebration with my family members, close friends and acquaintances to honor my blessings and give gratitude for my life."

We accepted without hesitation. Mrs. Trevor said to expect our official invitations in the mail.

We hugged and held each other closely for almost a minute.

That was the last time we gathered for our joyous wealth discussions.

Prologue

Mrs. Trevor's birthday party was held at a grand, luxurious banquet hall, with magnificent centerpieces on each table, sparkling chandeliers and tuxedoed waiters. Everyone from our group had dressed up beautifully for the occasion and brought their loved ones. Sarah was with her daughter Anusha and her partner. Georgina came with her two boys. A ravishing Terri arrived with her boyfriend. Nellie attended with her husband, her fitted dress proudly showing off her pregnancy.

We all mingled with Mrs. Trevor's family members, celebrated her eighty-five years and honored her life with toasts and speeches.

It was a joyous, emotional evening, and the last time we all gathered together. Mrs. Trevor died in peace a couple of days later.

Our group scattered, as everyone continued with their busy lives and journeys. I stayed in touch with each of them now and then.

Sarah told me that she and Georgina were present as per the lawyers' and the executors' invitation when they read Mrs. Trevor's last will and testament. At that meeting the executor gave Sarah a sealed letter Mrs. Trevor had written, telling her about her net worth with too many zeros to count and how they started with nothing. Sarah said Mrs. Trevor wanted to give her hope and remind her that anything is possible! Along with the letter was a trust document that Mrs. Trevor had set up for Anusha's education. I remember Sarah was in tears telling me how touched she was by the great gesture Mrs. Trevor had shown with a large sum left for Anusha as inheritance.

Children are our future, Mrs. Trevor always used to say.

Georgina also shared that Mrs. Trevor had set up a large trust fund for her son Eric. Georgina was zestful if a bit overwhelmed because Mrs. Trevor indicated in her letter that once Georgina completed her childhood education a medical and research clinic would be created, and Georgina would be the president running the clinic with total authority.

Georgina divorced her husband, was granted full custody of her children and received support for them.

Three years after Mrs. Trevor's death, a high tech clinic opened with the multimillions she had donated as a charitable gift. A monument was built in memory of Mrs. Trevor and Georgina was officially designated president of the clinic.

Sarah continued her education and worked part-time as a paralegal while living in a common-law relationship with her girlfriend and Anusha. A few years later she became a sought-after lawyer and married her love, her partner. When Sarah turned thirty-one she gave birth to a beautiful baby boy. The father was a good friend of her partner's. He gave up his rights as a parent, but they made an agreement so he could visit the boy.

Terri had found her prince charming, the really great man we had met at Mrs. Trevor's birthday party. She had fallen in love and softened up quite a bit. Four years after they met, they married. Terri's husband was not as rich as she was, and she didn't mind. Terri retired early at the age of fifty and travelled the world with her husband for six months.

After we met at the art gallery, Nellie had been very inspired and made a few dazzling, magnificent art pieces during her pregnancy. Later that year she gave birth to a healthy beautiful boy whom she adored. About four and a half years after the baby was born, she started taking additional courses in business and accounting and became more involved in her husband's business. By the time her boy was in middle school, she was head of the accounting department and her paintings were always exhibited at the gallery where we met.

As I reflect on this I smile in gratitude acknowledging my blessings and the gifts life has offered me.

When I think of how we all expanded and evolved I feel joyous and exultant.

I was able to share my knowledge and wisdom with these astonishing women, to discover their passions, joys and sorrows. As much as we had different lives and aspirations we all shared our vulnerabilities, our fears, and our spirits, with resilience and connection. I was elated to observe how each of these women achieved what they yearned for and were passionate about.

In honor of Mrs. Trevor I start with her. The number one priority in her circle of life was family. She forgave herself, accepting her daughter's death without blame and recognized that life has its own plan. She also included her grandchild in her will among others. It warms my heart to know she died in peace and without regret.

Terri's biggest fear was that she would not be able to share her life with anyone. She found her perfect partner and was able to retire early and travel the world.

Sarah's life expansion was impressive. She became an eminent lawyer and had a beautiful family. She even started taking dance classes as a hobby. All of the desires in her circle of life became a reality.

Nellie's wish was to have a baby and she was blessed with one. Her creativity blossomed and she was frequently commissioned to create unusual art and sculptures. Most importantly she was able to increase her wealth significantly by taking a leadership role in her husband's company.

I was enthralled by how Georgina became empowered by taking care of her own needs and well-being. She took inspired action and followed her heart for a worthy cause. Her actions led Mrs. Trevor to trust Georgina with her endowment. Georgina became a prominent force in medical research thanks to her power and empowerment.

Tears of joy run down my face. I know I had an impact on and I was impacted by these beautiful souls.

In the end it is all about love, nothing more and nothing less!

And life goes on…

Acknowledgements

For years I have been privileged to receive the teachings of **Yaz** (or Yahweh) channeled by **Charles Little,** to whom I am grateful for being the vessel that transmits the information. These teachings have become part of who I am today.

I acknowledge **Emiliya Zhivotovskaya,** founder of The Flourishing Centre, for her dedication to Positive Psychology, which I am fortunate to be certified in.

I was honored to be nominated by my client **Barbara Kobak** and be awarded Woman of Inspiration in 2019.

I acknowledge **Martin Sutherland,** a successful business owner, for being my longest standing loyal client.

I am grateful to **JT Foxx** and his team directed by **Francie Baldwin,** for introducing me to many celebrities and wealthy, successful entrepreneurs around the globe.

I am grateful to **Fred Fishback,** a self-made billionaire, for his time and advice. He repeatedly pointed out my uniqueness as an entrepreneur, and the methods I can contribute to my clients and to my business.

I acknowledge **Raymond Carmichael,** a successful entrepreneur client, for being supportive of my metaphysical talks and seminars when I started many years ago.

I am thankful to **Kevin France,** who encouraged me to quantum leap my business.

I acknowledge **Esma Gaudin,** who assured me I was capable of choreography when we started our first dance theatre production.

I am thankful to **Sarah Kutryk,** one of our original principal dancers whose creativity, energy and dedication was essential in the commencement of our dance theatre productions.

I am thankful to **Monica Kretschmer,** founder of Universal Womens Network, for inviting me to join the National Ambassadors of Canada and the selection committee for the Women of Inspiration award in 2020.

I recognize **Nicholas Stirling, Sherri Fetterly, Barry Waite** and **Meredith Wrede** for their support in our productions of Evolution Dance Theatre.

I acknowledge **Jason Gilbert** and **Reggie Batts** for their support in my business.

I am thankful to **Lisa Carter** for her gentle guidance in writing this book.

I acknowledge my publisher **Raymond Aaron** and his team for their assistance.

I am thankful to my sisters **Karine Hovsepian-Ruby** and **Adrineh Bennett** for their constant love and support.

I am grateful to all my clients, cast and crew members, audiences, readers and anyone I had the pleasure of crossing paths with, who contributed to my life journey in any shape or form.

With Gratitude
Armineh Keshishian

TRUTH

In the grandeur of things
Nothing matters, all passes
All that remains is beauty, pain
And then beauty
And life goes on to another cycle.

What matters is what you gave and
What you received,
The experiences you had
The beauty you had,
And what you portrayed and penetrated.

The compassion you had
The friends you made
The lives you changed and affected.

Nothing goes unnoticed in the book of life!

The feelings we share
The moments we share
Are never unnoticed.
They have an effect, an impact.
For what is the purpose of it all?
It seems the purpose is to give and to receive
And to feel and be felt,
To give an impact
And have an impact,
As life is created by such.

So be it! So beautiful and so perfect!

Armineh Keshishian
May 30, 2005 ©

Visit our websites:
www.JoyousWealth.com
www.WealthandWellnessGlobal.com
To receive a free colored copy of the *Joyous Wealth* Workbook
To take the free Wealth Consciousness Quiz
To participate in our seminars and retreats
To book a one-on-one or group coaching call
To invite Armineh Keshishian to speak at your event